Praise for *Transister*

"It's impossible not to admire Kate Brookes's moving portrait of her own transgender child blossoming into her own. *Transister* is the poignant story of a family finding its way in a world where gender identity can be a life and death matter. It's also a testament to the fearless determination of a mother to hold her family together in the face of misunderstanding and prejudice. This is an important book for anyone struggling to find their truest self—and for those who love them."

—Amy Ellis Nutt, Pulitzer Prize–winning journalist and author of *New York Times* bestseller *Becoming Nicole: The Transformation of an American Family*

"Every family is different. Every child is different. So, NO ONE is different. We are all unique individuals and as a parent in the same neighborhood, it's been beautiful to follow the transformation and transition and the confidence of Kate and her family. Most importantly, their 'transister' family doesn't even phase my boys. That's the world I want to continue to live in."

—Denise Albert, journalist, entrepreneur, advocate and founder of My Cancer Family (and formerly TheMOMS).

"Kate excavates a well-lit path for parents with a transgender child with her no-nonsense, down-to-earth style."

—Atoosa Rubenstein, former editor-in-chief of *Seventeen* magazine and founding editor of *CosmoGirl*

"As a mother, reading *Transister* feels like sitting across from Brookes in a cafe, drinking coffee and hanging on every word as she plainly and openly tells her story. She holds nothing back, sharing her truth with wit, warmth, and hard-earned wisdom. I found myself welling up with tears, laughing out loud and nodding my head in empathetic solidarity. Because to love a child is to want, more than anything, for that child to be authentically themselves—beautiful, complicated, wonderful—and for the world to not only accept them but to celebrate them. *Transister* is a gift to everyone—families who are navigating this journey, and all the allies who want to love and support them."

—Natalie Silverstein, author of *Simple Acts:*
The Busy Family's Guide To Giving Back

transister

Raising Twins in a Gender-Bending World

Kate Brookes

SHE WRITES PRESS

Published 2023
Printed in the United States of America

Print ISBN 978-1-64742-521-0
E-ISBN 978-1-64742-522-7
Library of Congress Control Number: 2023906796

For information, address:
She Writes Press
1569 Solano Ave #546
Berkeley, CA 94707

Interior Design by Kiran Spees

She Writes Press is a division of SparkPoint Studio, LLC.

For my children (aka A and B), who make my heart sing and make me prouder...and more exhausted than I ever thought possible.

Part One
My Twin Boys

1: Contemplator and Flailer

Before they were born, I'd unofficially named our twins Contemplator and Flailer. Contemplator was clearly laid-back and chill; I imagined him lying in my belly with his hand on his belly, enjoying the warmth of my womb, while contemplating current world (or, at the very least, fetal) events.

Flailer was the antithesis—moving and grooving almost constantly, kicking me in the ribs, the boobs, and the pubic bone, seemingly uncomfortable in such close quarters and trying to figure a way out. My coworkers would watch as Flailer created a moving bulge under my shirt during meetings, already much more entertaining than whatever video project we were supposed to be discussing.

Truth is, I was digging it. Despite my prior devotion to the gym, I welcomed my widening waistline and loved watching my abdomen morph into the crazy, gravity-defying, life-sustaining balloon it was becoming. Because as hard as I'd worked for my bathing suit body, I'd worked even harder for my pregnancy body.

Following seven rounds of fertility treatments, dozens of Lupron injections, endless pangs of jealousy (why was the whole Upper West Side pregnant except for me?), and, ultimately, eight excruciating weeks of bed rest, my dreams of motherhood were about to come true.

I'd wanted to have kids for as long as I could remember. I'd almost tried to have them with my first husband, when I was certainly more fertile and the pregnancy process would have been less complicated and more about having passionate sex than spreading my legs for a medical technician. But I'd known in my gut that Husband #1 and I weren't slated for the long haul, and I didn't want to bring children into a marriage destined for disaster. I'd seen how that worked out with my own parents, and I did *not* want to repeat the pattern.

My mom's multiple marriages, bouts with depression, and suicide attempts made my own childhood about as stable as a two-legged table. I remember being called to the principal's office in fifth grade. It had been one of "those mornings" in our house—my mom yelling, me crying, my brother and I barely making it to our respective bus stops. When my teacher picked up the classroom phone receiver at 9:23 a.m., glanced at me, and said, "I'll send her right down," I had a pit in my stomach. I was certain the police would be there, waiting to tell me my mom was dead, that I needed to go home. Instead, the school secretary handed me the phone from her desk and said, "Here, Katie, your mom says she needs to talk to you."

"Hi, Mommy," I said into the receiver.

"I'm sorry, Katie," she replied, her teary voice shaking ever so slightly. "I'm sorry this morning was so tough. It wasn't your fault. And I want you to know that I love you and am sorry for yelling at you and your brother."

I looked over at the secretary, who had an expectant look on her face.

"It's okay, Mommy; I love you too," I told her. Because (a) I *did* love her and (b) I knew that was what I was supposed to say. And if she couldn't do what was expected of a mom, I could at least do what I thought was expected of a kid: get perfect grades, stay out of trouble, and take care of her.

Almost thirty years later, I was determined to give my children the childhood I hadn't had, in a home filled with love, kindness, and a sense of normalcy, stability, and predictability—all the good words ending with "y." I talked to my belly every day, telling my twins how much I loved them, how much their daddy and I wanted them, how excited we were to meet them, and how we'd do everything in our power to make sure they felt safe and secure. That they would never feel like they had to fend for themselves.

And I wore my pregnancy like a badge. A really big badge that appeared to grow exponentially by the millisecond, attracting lots of attention and speculation along the way. It seemed everyone—friends, family, even strangers on the subway—knew exactly what genders our babies would be. What's more, they felt comfortable, even compelled, to share their less-than-scientific predictions with me.

"Your boobs and belly are really big, but you have no butt," the guy at the corner newsstand told me. "Definitely boys."

"Your cheeks look fatter when you smile; you are sooo carrying girls," my cousin said with conviction.

"One of each," my coworker promised. "Presto. Instant family. Done."

"All we really want is happy and healthy," I remember telling my best friend, Lauren, from college. "But if I'm being honest, I'm petrified of having girls."

Even *that* was an understatement. Girls reminded me of cats—moody, clawing for no reason, ready to pounce. I was fairly confident that if we had twin girls, their favorite color would be pink and their first word "ruffle." Which meant I'd have absolutely nothing in common with them, and that would suck. I'd never been a girlie girl—never felt I had the right clothes or the right hair, always felt like I was trying too hard and never quite fit in. Of course, I noticed that other girls had mothers who helped them—braided their hair, acknowledged their growth and the cut of their clothes, and made sure they had the things that would help them fit in. How could you fit in when you were worried someone was going to find out your mother was mentally ill?

As a little kid I could play baseball and football with the boys and no one questioned my appearance, but as I grew older, I always felt like the girls were sizing me up, like all of my and my family's flaws were being cataloged and counted against me.

No, the whole female dynamic was too fraught for me. I wanted boys.

‡ ‡

Fears aside, the months of my pregnancy were filled with endless expectations and anticipation. The bigger I grew, the bigger Contemplator and Flailer were growing, and that was the goal. My husband, Mike, and I had become slightly obsessed with birth weight after I was hospitalized at twenty-eight weeks for possible preterm labor, during which visit the NICU nurse had stood at my bedside rattling off the complications that could come from giving birth so early to babies that would likely weigh only a couple of pounds apiece.

After two days of being poked, prodded, and monitored around the clock, I, a former Jewish studies major who almost became a rabbi, had begun praying feverishly to the "please keep these babies inside me for a little longer" God.

The doctors at the hospital had given me firm, clear instructions upon my release: stay home and lie down on my side, legs raised, 24/7, except for going to the bathroom, taking a two-minute shower, or going to doctors' appointments, for which I was told I would need a wheelchair. At one of my bimonthly prenatal visits with my high-risk OB-GYN a few weeks later, I asked what would happen if I stood up, left my apartment, and walked around the block.

"The babies would probably come right out," he replied.

I had grand plans of using this forced "time-out" to brush up on my video-editing techniques, refresh my dwindling Hebrew skills, maybe even read some of the classics I'd overlooked in my school days. Instead, I lay in bed binge-watching *Mad Men* while trying to keep my legs closed.

"Remember, only get up if you really need to," Mike would tell me every morning while placing a huge jug of water next to me, reminding me to stay hydrated, and kissing me goodbye before heading to work.

"Got it," I'd say, feeling increasingly annoyed that he thought he needed to remind me to follow our doctor's orders—as if I'd even consider taking any unnecessary risks that might jeopardize the little people we'd worked so hard to create. But I sort of understood. I could tell that he felt scared and helpless. Unlike at work, where he planned, managed, and implemented million-dollar IT projects without breaking a sweat, he couldn't micromanage our pregnancy. It didn't matter how hard he worked or how much experience he had; when it came to my belly, all Mike could do was hope the babies continued baking.

My parents sounded concerned too. My dad and stepmom knew how much I wanted to be a mom and had been super supportive as Mike and I had trudged through the fertility process. My actual mom, meanwhile, had been in Florida for much of my pregnancy. Shortly after I'd announced we were having twins, she'd decided to leave the Northeast and "try something new" for a bit.

"How long do you think you'll be gone?" I'd asked her on one of our earlier phone calls. "Who are you staying with?"

"I'm not sure, and you don't know him," she told me.

"Oh. Do you think you'll be back by the time I give birth?"

Silence.

I hadn't told my mom about our fertility issues. Anytime she'd asked if we planned to have kids, I'd said, "Of course," and left it at that, not expecting a woman who'd drunk, smoked, and enjoyed her drugs (both prescribed and recreational) in her childbearing years and yet had still been able to get knocked up seemingly on demand to offer a sympathetic ear.

Nope. I would go this alone, as I always had: lying on my side for fifty-six straight days, praying I'd be able to do right by my kids.

‡ ‡

Somehow, I beat the odds: I lasted thirty-seven weeks and birthed almost fifteen pounds of baby. Baby boy, that is. (Chalk one up for the corner newsstand guy.) I was proud. Really proud. So proud that I didn't mind when my high-risk OB-GYN took most of the credit.

"I make big babies," he told me.

Contemplator, whom the doctors pulled out first and whom we named Jacob Alexander, continued to contemplate. He appeared relaxed, resigned, and content with the beautiful monotony of "eat, sleep, poop, and repeat" that is newborn life. He also seemed like he was in deep thought the whole time.

I wonder how many ounces of formula I'm drinking?

What's that cream they keep smearing on my tushie?

Why do I pee on that nice lady every time she takes off my diaper?

And . . .

What's up with the kid next to me screaming nonstop?

Because as uncomfortable as Gideon Andrew had seemed *inside* my belly, he seemed even more so *outside*. He didn't just cry to let us know he'd arrived—he flat-out wailed. I used to say that Gid, as we often called him, cried for his first eighteen months, but that's not entirely true. He didn't cry when he slept. But he also didn't sleep a lot.

"I've never seen a baby like this," one baby nurse told me the first day she started working with us.

"Interesting," I managed to say while thinking, *Why the hell would you say something like that?*

As it was, Mike and I were fairly clueless about the whole parenthood thing. Yes, I'd been a camp counselor, but always to the tweens. Most counselors found that age too bitchy to handle, but I'd requested them every summer. I knew the girls' tough facades only covered up their insecurities and angst, and I loved that I could break through their rough exteriors, letting them reveal their softer, kinder insides. Knowing how my own counselors had saved me as a kid, I'd made it my mission to be the counselor they could count on and come to when they were feeling down or lost. As for younger kids, my niece and nephew were my pride and joy. Still . . . two babies . . .

Mike was the last to get married among his circle of friends, and by the time we met, he was already an honorary "uncle" to a slew of kids; he'd become an expert at remembering birthdays and sending gifts. Still . . . two babies . . .

Yeah, so, it's probably not surprising that some of the hands-on stuff—the day-to-day, minute-to-minute acts of parenting—threw us both for a loop. The nurse at the hospital literally needed to show us how to change a diaper. (It didn't help that the sixteen-year-old sharing the room with us seemed like an expert.)

But as novice a parent as I was, I certainly didn't need our baby nurse—or anyone, for that matter—pointing out that one of my two beautiful, blue-eyed boys was almost constantly going ballistic. I could see it. And I could hear it. And I was living it. We all were.

Trying to interpret their differing demeanors into a "look" beyond calm versus inconsolable, I found myself dressing Jacob in softer, gentler outfits (light blues, pale yellows, a frog-patterned onesie that we received as a hand-me-down) and Gid in the more "manly" outfits—think bright, bold primary colors, newborn sports jerseys, onesies with slogans like "I'm a heartbreaker," and anything covered with fire trucks or baseballs. And why not? The outfits seemed to suit them. Jacob seemed soft and chill; Gideon looked like he was ready to battle the world. In retrospect, he probably was.

Case in point? Swaddling. We swaddled the kids before every nap and every bedtime, a strategy loosely defined as "wrapping up babies like burritos so they feel snuggly and safe." My guess, though, is Gid would have preferred the British definition of swaddling:

swaddling clothes (British) *1. Plural noun: restrictions or supervision imposed on the immature.*

I'm sure Gideon saw swaddling as the ultimate restriction. He'd wiggle and jiggle his little body through the entire swaddling process, as if fighting both the cloth and the person attempting to secure it.

To be clear, it's not like we were using an actual blanket and swaddling the kid from scratch the way they do in the hospital. That system entailed multiple steps of folding with near geometrical precision, and would have definitely driven me bonkers. Instead, we were using those precut, easy-to-use, adjustable, Velcro-strapped, you-can-swaddle-your-newborn-in-a-matter-of-seconds "swaddle sacks." Yet it still took us many minutes to swaddle him in and only a few seconds for him to wiggle, jiggle, and flail his way out. I started calling him "Houdini."

The fact was, Gideon just couldn't seem to get comfortable.

Ever.

We changed formulas.

We changed rash creams.

We changed outfits.

We rocked him, bounced him, sang to him, snuggled him, even tried to soothe him with the sounds of a hair dryer, which actually worked for a time. Unfortunately, anything that worked, anything that would calm him, only worked for a time.

I remember saying that he seemed genuinely uncomfortable in his own skin. Even my husband, who was reluctant to admit anything was wrong, ultimately admitted to our pediatrician—albeit years later—that Gid did appear to be "in moderate discomfort" much of the time.

It didn't take me years to notice. *What does Gideon need that we aren't giving him?* I wondered. *Is he screaming just to scream, or is he in pain? Is he trying to tell us something? And if so, what?* I projected a calm exterior, but some days I felt helpless and wondered if I was already messing up this mom thing.

‡ ‡

By the time the kids turned eighteen months, I was looking into getting Gideon evaluated by a developmental pediatrician. He seemed to maintain good eye contact. He was rolling over, crawling, and hitting most of his "baby milestones" at or near the suggested range. Over time, he'd developed the so-called pincer grasp and was able to place Cheerios in his mouth like a champ. So, I didn't think he was on the autism spectrum. Yet I knew in my heart that something about Gid was different.

But it was hard to convince Mike of the need. In fact, I think I even canceled the first appointment because he wasn't on board.

"He's just a regular kid," Mike would say. "Who happens to cry a lot and is a little uncomfortable. There is nothing wrong with him."

"I'm not saying there's something *wrong* with him," I pleaded. "I just want to know how we can *help* him."

Because with every day that passed, I felt like I was watching the vow I had made slip away. I couldn't help him, and I needed to know *why*. Why Gideon arched his back and screamed bloody murder when we tried to strap him into his double stroller.

Why he squirmed, flailed, and hit me when I tried to cut his toenails.

Why he wouldn't go into the sandbox with his brother.

Why he got so agitated over seemingly nothing that he'd hit himself, wail out loud, scratch his face and body, and end up bright red, bruised, and battered.

And I wanted to know what we could do so Gideon would stop doing all of these things and just enjoy being a little person.

I'm not sure how long the doctor planned to observe our son after I finally convinced Mike that *one appointment* would be a good thing. But I do remember that about twenty minutes into our visit, Gideon lost it.

He'd done fine playing with the blocks, responding to the doctor's various prompts, and being the generally delicious toddler we knew and loved. But then it was like someone flipped a switch. He arched his back. He started crying. And screaming. Loudly. Continuously. With no end in sight. He arched his back even more, pushing himself back so far that I had to catch him to make sure he didn't slam his head into a bookcase.

I hugged him.

I kissed him.

I gently bounced him.

Nothing helped.

Finally, the doctor said this was getting dangerous, that Gideon could hurt himself, and she asked Mike to take him to the waiting room so she and I could talk. She'd send us her report soon, she told me, but it was clear that Gideon had some sensory processing issues and would likely benefit from early intervention, or EI, as it was known. Some occupational therapy, she said; perhaps some speech therapy too.

My mind was racing. My heart seemed to be pounding a thousand beats per second.

"Your son drools a lot," she said. "He also has a difficult time making his sounds, let alone repeating words." The words that most kids his age, including his twin brother, were already saying and repeating with apparent ease.

I walked out of the exam room with the doctor, shook her hand, and said thank you. Mike, holding on to a slightly less agitated Gideon, stood up, looked at me, and thanked the doctor as well.

I hugged Gid, and Mike and I walked him toward the elevator, each of us holding one of his little hands, wondering what would come next.

"I see it, babe," Mike said after we stepped inside and helped Gid press the button to the lobby. "I do see it now."

I sighed. And tried to hold back my tears.

"I'm not looking for things to be wrong, Mike," I whispered. "I just want us to help Gideon be more comfortable in his skin."

"I know, Katie," he said. "I do too."

I looked back down at Gid and smiled at my little man. His laugh, which he did use when he wasn't crying, was infectious. And I genuinely loved playing with, being with, and caring for him and his bro, even though I could tell that our day-to-day existence was a little louder, a tad more tumultuous, and slightly more complicated than that of our friends with similar-aged children, even the ones with twins.

But these were the kids we'd birthed. They were all we knew. And we loved them, we were proud of them, and we loved being their parents. Still, I had this gnawing feeling that something else was going on, something bigger than just the sensory stuff.

I promised myself that Mike and I would do everything within our power to make sure they'd both be okay.

2: Therapy Times Two

"Mommy, Mommy, come!" Jacob heard me walk in the apartment the moment I opened the door and immediately screamed out from the bathroom.

The twins weren't quite two yet; I was still working full time for a marketing production company and traveling almost once a week. But if there was even a remote possibility that I could make it home in time for their baths, I'd fly out of the office to do it.

"What's up, kiddos?" I asked, swapping places with our nanny and helping to lather them up.

"Mommy, look!" Gideon said, pointing to the heart he'd drawn on the tub wall with his bath crayons.

"So pretty; I love it, babe!" I said, planting a kiss on his sudsy head. "And what about you, Super J? Tell me what you drew!"

"I drew a truck," Jacob, who was still talking in more complete sentences than Gideon, told me. "And a big pile of dirt. My truck dig it."

"Your truck dug it?" I said. "That's amazing. It must be a really strong truck. I love both of your pictures."

The kids splashed around together, taking turns pouring a Tupperware bowl full of water on each other's head. I'd heard you could go online and buy an official shampoo rinse cup for kids, but I subscribed more to the one-plastic-cup-is-as-good-as-another philosophy. Besides, the kids thought it was funny that we used food containers in the bath.

"Ouch!" Jacob screamed.

"What's wrong, baby?"

"Giddy pulled my penis!"

"Boys," I said, trying to stifle a laugh, "you may pull on your own penis, but you may not pull on your brother's. How was school?" I asked, trying to change the subject.

"Good," they said in unison.

"Great to hear," I said, hoping that was the case.

The boys had been having a little "trouble" in school lately. It had never occurred to me that this was possible in preschool, but I was learning. Quickly.

The kids had been accepted into the only Reform Jewish day school in NYC, a not-small coup. But now, just a few months into the academic year, I feared the school was second-guessing its decision. Jacob and Gideon were in the same two's class three hours twice a week, under the care of two full-time teachers and several "floaters." Floaters, as the name suggested, floated among classes on an as-needed basis. Our class had reportedly needed more floaters as the school year progressed.

I drained the bathtub, dried off the kids, helped put them in their jammies, and sat them in front of a Melissa & Doug nesting toy so I could talk to our nanny.

"How was today?" I asked her.

"Ehh," Olivia replied. A recent college grad, Olivia was getting her master's degree online in special education. "The teachers didn't look so happy when I picked them up from class. But honestly, they never seem really happy to see me."

"Right." I sighed. "Did they say anything specific?"

"I asked how the day went and got a sort of eye roll, headshake in response."

"Fabulous," I said, looking over at my little men and watching them work together to try to stack the numbered cardboard boxes.

We'd received several emails from the teachers and a call from the nursery division director in the past two weeks alone.

‡ ‡

Gid was having trouble transitioning from one activity to the next and would often tantrum between art and story time, or music and free play. His new occupational therapist, who he'd begun seeing after his developmental evaluation, explained that transitions could be especially difficult for kids with sensory issues. She promised they were working on it during their twice-weekly sessions, as was Tali, his speech pathologist, who I referred to as the "Gideon whisperer."

Gideon seemed to have a "thing" for Tali. His little face would light up when he saw her walk up the steps from the sensory gym to retrieve him from the waiting room. Even if he was in the middle of a mega-meltdown.

"What's going on here, Gideon?" she asked in a firm but loving voice when she saw me sprawled on the floor one afternoon, struggling to unzip his jacket, as he screamed, arched his back, and flailed in my arms.

She kneeled down, her beautiful blue eyes looking directly into Gideon's own baby blues. "This behavior is not okay. You know you need to take off your jacket and socks before you come downstairs to see me. This is what we do before every class. Let's go, Gideon. You can do this."

And just like that, Gid stopped flailing and started to settle himself. I wasn't sure if I was more grateful or embarrassed that our twenty-something therapist could do, with seemingly little effort, what I was clearly incapable of. But I welcomed the reprieve and watched somewhat admiringly as she took his hand and they walked downstairs.

I often chatted with the other moms whose kids were downstairs receiving their state-mandated therapies during Gideon's sessions. Sometimes we compared notes.

"Does your son scream a lot?" I asked a woman named Melanie, who was becoming a friend.

"Only when he's awake," she said, and we both laughed.

"Is that your kid or mine?" we'd take turns asking when we heard a yell we couldn't quite identify coming from downstairs. Nine out of ten times, we quickly learned, it was one of our sons making the noise, even though there were generally five to six other kids in the sensory gym with them.

Occasionally, I was invited down to see what Gideon was doing.

"Weeeeeee!" Gideon would shout with a smile as his therapist pushed him in the sensory swing—a fabric cocoon that dangled from the ceiling on a rope. His little body swung back and forth, his smile widening with each push.

The first time I saw Gid swinging, I'll admit I was confused, but his therapist set me straight. "The vestibular system," she told me, "is the most important of the body's senses. It tells us if we're moving, how fast we're moving, and in which direction we're headed." When kids have a regularly developed vestibular system, she explained, they can navigate their environment with confidence, because their brain knows exactly where the body is in relation to other objects.

"Children with sensory issues, however," she continued, "often have vestibular dysfunction and don't move as confidently. It's almost as if their bodies don't know their exact location in space."

With each swinging motion, Gideon's view of the room changed. He could feel the wind against his face and maybe even butterflies in his stomach. His brain began to tell him, "Okay, the view of the room is changing, I feel butterflies, so I must be swinging."

The swing was also designed to improve his balance and coordination, strengthen his muscles, and act as a mood booster. The latter was pretty obvious. The fact that my kid went from screaming and flailing to giggling and smiling in a matter of minutes made me an instant believer.

When Gideon completed a task successfully at therapy, he'd receive a prize. Usually a sticker (he favored the hearts, rainbows, and princesses) or, if he was super lucky, a few minutes to play with Tali's hair.

"I hairdresser," my little guy would say. "I make hair pretty."

Somehow, he seemed happiest and most relaxed at therapy when he was touching, playing with, and doing what he referred to as "stylin'" Tali's hair. For her part, Tali reported that she got a ton of language out of Gideon during these styling sessions. I didn't quite understand the science behind this one, but if braiding hair and practicing ponytails helped his speech improve, who was I to complain?

‡ ‡

With Tali's help, Gideon seemed to be improving, at least as far as the rate of emails from his teacher was an indication. So, the phone call regarding Jacob's behavior definitely caught us off guard.

I was in Washington, DC, at the time, waiting for my crew to finish setting up the lights for an impending interview with the CEO of a Fortune 100 company, when the school number popped up on my cell phone.

"Hi, this is Kate," I said, trying to sound cheerful.

"Hi, Kate, this is Shelley, from Jacob's school. Jacob is okay," she said, prompting me to let out an audible sigh of relief. "But," she continued, and my chest started to tighten, "he just attacked a classmate."

"He *attacked* someone?" I half asked, half repeated, a bit too loudly. "Is the kid okay? Is Jacob okay? What happened?"

"Everyone is okay," the head of the preschool continued, "but Anna was pretty upset. The teachers tell me Jacob pulled her hair for no reason. It took both of them to pull Jacob off of her."

"Yikes," I responded, unsure of what else to say.

I could feel my face getting red; my cameraman motioned at me to see if I wanted him to leave the room to give me some time alone. I did not. All I wanted was for my kids to go to school, make friends, learn some things along the way, and fit in with other kids—just like the other kids. Why was this all so hard? What was I doing wrong?

Shelley and I chatted for a couple more minutes, my mind racing the whole time—part wishing I could be there to cuddle my son, tell him I loved him, and let him know everything was going to be okay, and part hoping Anna's family didn't think my kid was some lunatic or, even worse, that my husband and I didn't know how to raise our children. Shelley and I decided I'd call Anna's mom to apologize personally, and we collectively hoped the incident was a one-off.

It wasn't.

Ultimately, I ended up needing to call Anna's mom again. And then a third time.

The hair-pulling incidents and a few other factors prompted us to get Jacob evaluated as well. The results? He was a sensory kid too. He just displayed different symptoms than his bro. Jacob also lacked core strength, which was why he often walked holding objects (or Anna's hair) to steady himself.

Unlike many new parents, I was familiar with sensory processing disorder (SPD) even before we received the diagnosis. Years earlier, I had helped media train one of the foremost thought leaders in SPD to prepare her for a series of radio and TV interviews. Once my boys were diagnosed, though, I learned more.

The Star Institute for Sensory Processing Disorder defines SPD as "a neurophysiological condition in which sensory input, either from the environment or from one's body, is poorly detected, modulated, or interpreted and/or to which atypical responses are observed." In practical terms, people with SPD have a hard time coping with the information from their senses—quite literally, what they see, smell, hear, taste, or touch. Loud noises could set off a sensory kid, for example, or a clothing label could make them feel so uncomfortable they'd be unable to sit still or pay attention.

Symptoms, I learned, are often age related. Infants and toddlers might have problems calming themselves; they can appear extremely irritable when being dressed and/or arch their back away from the person holding them. Classic Gideon. Preschoolers often have difficulty performing fine motor skills, they might invade other people's space and touch/grab everything around them (e.g., Anna's hair), and they're likely to experience sudden mood changes and tantrums. Classic Jacob.

The studies vary, but most suggest at least one in twenty people are affected by SPD. These numbers increase dramatically in people with autism or ADHD. Occupational therapy (OT), physical therapy (PT), and speech therapy can help mitigate the symptoms, especially when the disorder is identified early on. Hence our twice-weekly appointments with the specialists at a sensory gym in our neighborhood—where, only six months after Gideon was diagnosed, Jacob joined the ranks of EI recipients.

Part of me was relieved. Mike and I now knew what we were dealing with, and we not only knew *how* to help our kids but also had access to the resources we needed—and just four blocks away, no less! Easy for me or our nanny to take both kids in our double stroller.

Except on those days when Gideon screamed, cried, and threw a tantrum as I tried strapping him into the stroller. Those moments were a particular kind of hell for me. I smiled, tried to maintain my composure, and tried to comfort him. "It's okay, little man," I'd say. "We're just going to see Tali. You love Tali!" Or "I know you'd probably rather stay home right now, but you can do this, kiddo! I know you can. Let's hop in the stroller, okay, buddy?"

"Okay."

That's all I wanted. For Gideon and Jacob to be "okay." Yet increasingly *I* was feeling anything but okay.

"Do you really think the kids need all this therapy?" Mike would ask me from time to time.

"Yeah, I really do," I'd tell him.

"How do we know it's even working?" he'd ask. "Can we prove the kids are making any more progress than they would without the therapy?"

"Can we prove that my being on bedrest made the kids stay in my belly any longer than they would have without that?" I asked.

"Good point," he admitted. "But I still think this is a lot of therapy for two-year-olds. My guess is they'd grow out of any of these issues over time."

"Maybe, maybe not. But I'm not willing to risk it."

For two reasons. One, I'm not wired that way; I couldn't just sit back and watch them flounder. And two, I was determined to make good on my promise to give them the normal childhood I'd missed.

Mike said his own childhood had been relatively normal—or "standard regular," as he referred to it. And by comparison, I couldn't disagree. Two parents, one marriage (at least during Mike's formative years), a house in Westchester, and one brother seven years his junior. Both kids growing up knowing they were loved and not having to worry about a parent killing herself. On paper, it was indeed relatively normal. It wasn't until Mike had graduated college that his parents parted ways and he found himself in the middle of a nasty divorce, during which he largely sided with his mom and took on a role (confidant, financial planner, and intermediary) that no child—even an adult one in his midtwenties—should ever assume.

I maintained that Mike's childhood wasn't quite as normal as he believed, that he either didn't see some significant issues (e.g., infidelity, financial issues, abusive behaviors) or that his parents swept them under the carpet until they created an ugly bulge that was impossible to ignore. Sometimes I wondered if Mike's upbringing prevented him from seeing—at least initially—the issues I did when it came to our kids. Not because he was trying to sweep them under the rug, but because that's what he was used to families doing: only seeing what they wanted to see.

‡ ‡

Meanwhile, I felt like I was working four full-time jobs—producer, wife, mother, and parent advocate, the last of which was often the most challenging. I was particularly grateful that my boss trusted my work ethic and knew I'd never let down a client or our company. Not once did he question why I spent so much time on the phone, talking about things that were clearly not production related.

Between setting up therapies, following up with therapists to monitor the kids' progress, doing their daily exercises with them, and filling out healthcare claims, I felt like I needed an extra me just to come close to staying on top of it all.

I couldn't imagine my mother ever going to bat for me in this way. She'd always seemed more concerned with the latest fads of the '70s—aerobics, the grapefruit diet, or sunning herself with those reflective mirrors in our backyard—than she had with how I was feeling. It was my dad who used to walk me back to my bedroom after having a bad dream. He'd tuck me in and sing me songs from *Peter Pan* or *West Side Story* until I fell back asleep.

If only my boys' issues could be fixed with show tunes. Instead, I suspected the OT, PT, and speech therapy were here to stay. Whatever it would take for them to be able to walk into a playground six months—a year?—from now and simply blend in.

3: Cinderella, Iron Man, and Naked Barbie

One piece of parenting advice: should the opportunity ever arise, never dress your sensory toddler in one-piece, fake fur, hooded animal costumes. No matter how cute you think they'll look as a miniature giraffe or lion, it's simply not worth the discomfort for the kids *or* for you when you're left dealing with an overheated, agitated, pint-size mini-beast.

We learned that lesson the hard way early on and planned subsequent Halloween costumes accordingly.

Baseball players. That's what the boys would be for Halloween number two. Regular clothes with a Yankees jersey and hat for Jacob, Mets for Gideon. Sounded easy enough, and it was . . . for a while. I even snapped a couple of happy pictures around 4:00 p.m. at our friend's party that I eventually emblazoned on various keychains and mugs to hand out as gifts. But just thirty minutes into the party, Mets boy was getting a little grumpy.

"Of course he's upset," I said to my husband. "He's wearing the wrong team."

We lasted longer at that year's party, but still—not long.

Halloween, I thought. *Highly overrated.*

‡ ‡

23

Not to my kids, though. By midsummer of the following year, at about age three and a half, they were already talking about costumes.

"Maybe I'll be Superman," Jacob said, throwing his arms out in front of him as though he were flying. "Or Lightning McQueen. Maybe even Mater." He was starting to get really excited.

"Maybe I'll be Batman," Gideon chimed in. "Or Sleeping Beauty!"

Jacob's eyebrows furrowed, and he looked as though he was in deep thought. Then, moments later, "Why would Giddy want to be Sleeping Beauty?" he wondered aloud.

Neither Mike nor I responded.

Our boys were smack dab in the middle of their Disney phase, and Mike and I were happy to fuel the fire. I'd recently returned from one of my West Coast treks, where I'd been producing a video about the making of Disney's Cars Land. My biggest corporate client had provided tons of technology for the new Pixar-inspired area of the park, and I'd spent several days filming its progression. I'd also received lots of swag from the grand opening—*Cars* T-shirts, Lightning McQueen stuffies, Mickey Mouse ears, and a princess doll for Gideon. He liked *Cars* and all . . . but he was *really* starting to dig the Disney princesses.

At home, Gid had begun collecting ceramic princesses that he painted at birthday parties. We usually went to at least one a weekend—at the bouncy place, kids' gym, or crafts center. Living in a city where the average family home tops out at 1,200 backyard-less square feet, party venues are a necessity. And there weren't that many to choose from at this age, so unless a parent got super creative and found an indoor animal farm (which one family did), most weekends found the boys decorating mugs, cartoon characters, and figurines at the various "paint your own pottery" places.

Jacob painted a slew of baseball players, sports cars, and ball-shaped piggy banks. Color selection wasn't important to him—nor was which hand he used to hold the brush. He just chatted with his buddies while haphazardly slopping on so many layers of paint that his creations were often the last ones in the group to dry.

Gideon, on the other hand, took almost as much time selecting his ceramics as he did painting them.

"I take rainbow," he'd say to the party lady at the craft store when it was his turn to choose a piece to paint. "Wait, can I have a heart?"

He'd then walk back to the paint table, heart in hand, and plop down among his favorite group of girls. (By this point Gideon spent most of his time with the little ladies, who seemed genuinely happy hanging with him.) Moments later, he'd invariably grab his heart and walk back to the ceramic selection area for a last-minute swap. He'd then rejoin his girls with a Rapunzel, Sleeping Beauty, Ariel, or whatever Disney princess the place had on hand.

Sometimes I wondered what the other moms thought when Gideon sat down, looking adoringly at Sleeping Beauty, seemingly transfixed by her ceramic curls. Did they suspect anything was different about my son? Did they notice he was the only *boy* painting a *girl*?

I noticed. And I couldn't help but think of that song they used to sing on Sesame Street: *"One of these things is not like the others . . ."*[1]

I didn't mind that Gideon wasn't like the other kids at the party. It was the rest of the song that gave me pause: *"One of these things just doesn't belong . . ."*

The song made me anxious. For me and for my son. Would Gideon *not* belong, I wondered? Did he already feel different from the other kids? Especially the boys his age?

I couldn't help but think of myself when I was a little kid. By today's standards, I'd surely have been considered gender nonconforming. I played mostly with boys; wore jeans, cutoffs, and boxy T-shirts; despised dresses; and readily chose GI Joe over Barbie. And as much as I liked riding Big Wheels with my best friend, Mark, and chasing the garbage men down our block, I didn't like when some of the girls on our dead-end street made fun of me for it. The only thing

I hated more than being told to put on a skirt to go to synagogue was being called a tomboy.

Why did my love of sports make me any less of a girl? Why did anyone care if I preferred digging in the dirt to playing hopscotch?

But it didn't seem like the other kids at the birthday party—or their parents—were looking at Gideon strangely when he painted his princesses. And Gideon, for his part, was smiling, chatting with his girlfriends, and appearing happy as a clam.

‡ ‡

I don't think any of us was super surprised when, as the next Halloween rolled around, Jacob picked out an Iron Man costume and Gid grabbed a Cinderella off the shelf.

"I want this," he said, handing me the bag.

"Wow, Cinderella!" I said. "Cool!" And then, "Are you sure you don't want to be Lightning McQueen or maybe Cookie Monster?"

"I want to be Cinderella," he persisted.

I paused, then swallowed. "Okay, love, Cinderella it is! I'm sure you'll be the best Cinderella out there." As we stood in line at the checkout counter, I wondered if anyone noticed that one of my two little boys was clutching a princess costume as though it were a life preserver.

Maybe it was.

‡ ‡

Later that night, Mike and I both admitted privately that we were worried. We wondered if I should have pushed Cookie, Lightning, or even a clown costume.

"I'm sure it'll be okay," we both agreed.

"But next year," Mike added, "I think we should steer him away from girls' costumes."

"I'm not sure I agree," I said, despite my obvious discomfort. "Besides, next year is a long time away."

‡ ‡

And this year, he was certainly the cutest and most original Cinderella in our playroom. Definitely the only one with short hair. And the only one wearing a long-sleeved gray T-shirt and blue jeans under the light blue dress with its two strings of pearls and a Cinderella cameo sewn on.

My mom, the kids' safta (Hebrew for grandma), thought it was "awesome" that Gideon dressed as a princess.

"His cousin used to play dress-up all the time when he was little," she reminded me on the phone that afternoon. "He loved that pink tutu so much in preschool that your brother started to worry."

"Oh, I remember," I replied, trying my best to sound upbeat and refusing to give any hints that I was concerned.

I was more forthcoming when I called my dad and stepmom. "God, I hope he doesn't get laughed at later today," I admitted a few minutes before bringing the kids to our building's party.

"If anyone laughs, you can tell them exactly where to go," my dad said.

"Okay, Padre," I said sarcastically. "I'll just let any four-year-old who messes with my kid have it. Especially if their parents or nanny are close by. 'Cause that'll go over super well."

"Gideon will be fine," my stepmom jumped in. "Just be sure to take plenty of pictures of him and Jacob, okay? We need some new ones of them in our living room."

‡ ‡

At the party, I used humor to deflect my misgivings.

"He looks so cute," a friend in the playroom said when we walked in.

"Yeah, it was either Cinderella or the Incredible Hulk," I replied. "We flipped a coin."

A few kids stared at Gideon, but if he minded, he didn't say anything.

"Where are the boys?" another friend asked when she saw me standing seemingly kidless next to the adult beverage table.

"J's over there with Max." I pointed. "The Iron Man playing basketball. And Gideon is the Cinderella in the playhouse with Julia."

"Cinderella?" she said with a smile. "That's awesome."

"Yup, keeping it real. You know we're a little gender-bendy in our home."

Not sure exactly what I meant by that. Or if it was entirely true. But it sounded good. And it stopped further questions. Besides, my description certainly wasn't inaccurate. Gideon loved playing dress-up at home and school, and especially at my mom's house. Even Jacob got in on the action sometimes. One of my favorite pics of the boys is of them dancing in her living room, Gideon wearing some fabulous bright green sequin dress and Jacob rocking a tutu. When I snapped the pic, I remember thinking it would be an awesome addition to their bar mitzvah montage, which I'd admittedly begun producing in my head eleven years before the presumed big day.

And both kids' favorite color at this time was pink. I'm pretty certain Jacob loved pink primarily because he loved his new buddy, Henry, who was the de facto mayor of his class. And Henry's favorite color was pink. Gid had liked pink for a while, and he wasn't even in Henry's class. We'd separated the kids after a first rocky year in the "twos," when we'd determined it was best for them, their classmates, their teachers, and our collective future at our Jewish day school if we pulled them apart. Anyway, liking pink wasn't considered odd for boys at this age.

But wearing a Cinderella costume still seemed somewhat avant-garde.

‡ ‡

One day around this time, I found Gideon sorting through boxes that big cousin Harper had shunned to the side of her bedroom. Harper's Barbie bins were overflowing with Malibu, Fashionista, Ballet, Graduation, City, and a bunch of other Barbies whose names we could only guess. But Gideon's favorites were the Naked Barbies. He dressed them, undressed them, changed their outfits, put up their hair, made them twirl and dance, lifted their arms, looked at their boobs, and ultimately left them naked.

When we left our cousins' home that afternoon, Gideon clutched his newfound treasure. Four Barbies. Three wearing some combination of pink and purple prom dresses, yoga outfits, and short shorts with high heels, and one wearing nothing at all.

Once home, Gideon cleared out a corner in the room he shared with Jacob and propped up the dolls for all to see.

"Those are so stupid," Jacob would say. "Why do you like Barbies so much? Don't you know they're for girls?"

"Anyone can play with Barbies," I interjected each time the conversation arose. "There's no such thing as girl toys or boy toys. They're just toys."

"Well, *I'm* not playing with Barbies," Jacob replied.

"And I *am*," Gid offered.

"That's great," I said. "You can play with them, Gid, and you don't have to, J-man. It's all good!"

And it was all good; I really did believe that. Who cared what my kids played with? Who cared what *anyone's* kids played with?

‡ ‡

Except many people *did* care.

Just ask Grayson Bruce, the nine-year-old boy who'd recently been bullied by classmates at his elementary school in Candler, North Carolina, for bringing a My Little Pony backpack to school. Rather than support Grayson and punish the bullies, his parents said the district had forbidden him from bringing the backpack to school altogether.[2]

I remember watching the *Today Show* in shock. *Could this actually happen in 2014?* I wondered.

The expert who weighed in on the matter pointed out the egregiousness of the response and agreed that if the school actually reacted this way, "that's placing the blame on the kid." Sandra

Graham, a professor of education at the University of California, Los Angeles, who studies the long-term effects of bullying, continued, "The principal is basically saying you brought this on yourself, so deal with it, as opposed to putting the responsibility back on the perpetrators."

A better response, Graham explained, would have been to use the incident as a teachable moment, one that would involve the whole school community working to change the climate and culture in the school.

While I was well aware that rural North Carolina was very different from my children's New York City bubble, the incident did make me wonder whether Gideon would be bullied for his taste in toys. That said, my more immediate concern was that Gideon's Barbies clearly made Jacob upset.

"Mom, he keeps leaving his stupid dolls on my bed," Jacob complained just weeks after the Barbies invaded their bedroom. "It's embarrassing. It's my room too, you know!"

"Gideon, baby," I said, acknowledging Jacob's point of view but still trying to play down the doll part, "please remember to keep your toys on your own bed and your own side of the room. Your bro doesn't leave his stuff in your area. Let's be considerate of each other's space, okay, love?"

"Okay, Mama," G replied as he continued dressing and undressing his Barbie.

‡ ‡

Soon, G began requesting new Barbies so he could start his own collection. At first, we used the Barbies as rewards: any time he completed one of the "behavior charts" we routinely plastered on the bedroom wall, he received a Barbie for his efforts.

In addition to OT, PT, and speech, we had now added a "feelings doctor" to our growing list of therapists.

"Charts are a great way to track behavior, reward positive efforts, and help create healthy behavioral patterns," the kids' feelings doctor had told us.

She seemed to be right.

In the beginning, the promise of a truck for Jacob or a Barbie for Gideon went a long way toward encouraging the boys to fill their charts by, for example, using their words instead of their hands, practicing first-time listening, and saying "please" and "thank you." Though, to be honest, Mike and I often lacked the consistency needed to keep the charts current. Between the twins' various early intervention therapies, wrangling with insurance, preschool, playdates, and our own full-time jobs, Mike and I were having a hard time keeping our heads above water, let alone remembering to fill out charts.

During this time, Mike and I often joked that we were clearly "that family"—the one with at least one crying toddler flopped on the ground, face-down, in the middle of the grocery store aisle, and the one that seldom made it through a full meal in a restaurant, even the most kid-friendly one. (I quickly lost track of how many eat-in experiences unexpectedly became takeout.)

As we entered the last year of preschool, though, despite the chaos that clouded our days, eventually the phone calls and emails from school subsided, the offers for playdates multiplied, and our family of four settled into something that could be described loosely as a routine.

Jacob's car collection grew, he continued trying new sports, and he loved being read to . . . and pretending to read books on his own.

G's Barbie bins multiplied, he started trying on my dresses at home, and when we walked down the street together, he'd frequently point to women's feet, exclaiming, "Heels! Flats! Heels! Flats!" much to the chagrin of passersby.

Did I think it was different, even a little odd, that Gideon was the only four-year-old boy I knew who was obsessed with Barbies? Of course I did. Did I suspect that G's affinity for all things pink and purple was less about color preference and more about gender iden-tity? Absolutely.

But if he was happy, we were happy. And Mike and I did our best to follow his lead. Mostly.

4: Princess Pressure

I remember the first time I drew a line in the sand. We'd just moved into the apartment next door—it was slightly larger than the one we'd been living in, though the twins would still be sharing a bedroom. Their "big boy" platform beds had arrived the previous week, the painters had just finished laying the final coat of sky blue on their walls, and new comforters would pull the room together while also giving the kids a chance to exert a little decision-making power in their often preplanned lives.

Olivia and I walked up and down the aisle at Bed Bath & Beyond while Jacob made a beeline for a racetrack comforter set, complete with steering wheel pillow and victory flag–covered sheets.

"I want this one, Mama," he cried out, lifting up the big bedding bag and wobbling toward me and our shopping cart.

"Super cute, my love," I had to admit. "And it will look so handsome in your new room." And then, "What about you, G? Which ones do you like?"

That's when I saw my little man staring, ostensibly starstruck, his eyes glued to Ariel, Sleeping Beauty, Cinderella, Mulan, Tiana, all of them, set upon a plush purply pink backdrop. It was his Disney dream come true, smack dab on one comforter in the middle of Aisle 3.

"Mama, look," he screamed. "Princesses!"

"Wow," I said, stealing a side glance at Olivia, who had lifted her hand to her mouth and was trying not to laugh. "That's sure a lot of princesses, sweetheart," I agreed.

"I want this!"

I don't want this. The thought jumped into my brain, unbidden.

I felt my face starting to get flushed, my armpits starting to dampen. *Why can't he just pick a regular comforter?* I wondered. *Why does everything need to be so complicated?*

My little guy bent down and kissed Cinderella, then glanced toward me expectantly.

"Oh man," I finally eked out, feigning disappointment. "The pink-and-purple background won't match your blue walls. Bummer. Let's see if we can find something else that goes."

And just like that, I took my visibly disappointed son's hand and dragged him toward the dinosaurs.

‡ ‡

"I just couldn't do it," I said to Mike that night as we checked in on the boys, Jacob sound asleep holding on to his steering wheel pillow, Gideon wrapped in a Tyrannosaurus rex and Velociraptor–clad quilt, fingers still clutching a naked Barbie. "I know he wanted the princess set, but it's Jacob's room too. And I didn't think it would be fair."

"I don't disagree, Katie," he reassured me. "I wouldn't have let him get that one either. I think you did the right thing."

I nodded. But I wasn't so sure.

I tossed and turned for much of the night. Did Gideon really believe we didn't buy the princess comforter because it didn't match his new room? He hadn't mentioned anything about it when we got home that afternoon. But I kept replaying the incident at the store over and over in my mind—each time seeing his big, wide smile turn into a frown and watching that pure childhood excitement leave his eyes when I said "no." How many other times, I wondered, had I denied his wants and wishes because they didn't align with my—or society's— expectations? *But we let the kid dress as Cinderella for Halloween,* I reminded and reassured myself; that had to mean we were supportive parents, right?

Then I thought back to the boys' last birthday party. We had long ago agreed that, despite sharing my womb and their birthday, the twins should never share a cake. Each kid should have their own personally curated and designed pastry with their own candles to blow out. Easy enough. Or so we thought.

It's not that we didn't *want* to get Gideon the Barbie cake he requested. It's more like we were *scared* to get him a Barbie cake. Or a Cinderella cake. Or a Rapunzel cake.

Scared of what? I'm not entirely sure. Maybe that some kid might laugh at G on his special day and make him feel "less than." Or, even worse, that a parent might say something derogatory, not only making fun of our son but also questioning my parenting and making *me* feel "less than."

Ultimately, Jacob settled on a football theme and G, after some initial reluctance, wound up with hearts and flowers. If partygoers or their parents thought that was odd, they sure didn't say anything to us. In fact, much of the hubbub at cake time was spent cleaning up after a kid who tossed his cookies about six minutes after the boys blew out their candles.

Would anything have turned out differently, I wondered, if Gideon had blown out his candles on a Cinderella cake? He'd sure seemed happy enough when he saw the hearts and flowers. Much like he'd seemed happy enough clutching his Barbie at bedtime earlier tonight in his newly decorated bedroom. But would happy "enough" be enough for Gideon?

‡ ‡

A couple months later, on a chilly Saturday afternoon in January, I was hanging out with the kids in our building's playroom. G was playing with his Barbies, Jacob was playing Nerf basketball, and our babysitter had just arrived. Mike and I were scheduled to drive to Long Island that night for a friend's fiftieth surprise birthday party, and I knew I'd better go upstairs soon to shower and get ready. But I was having fun watching and playing with my boys and wanted to stay a little bit longer.

I had just started running after a kid—I can't recall which one—when my phone rang. I looked down at the screen to see a New Jersey number, one I didn't recognize. Normally I'd let it go to voice mail. But somewhat instinctively, I picked up after the second ring.

"Hi, this is Kate," I said.

"Hi, Kate, it's Frank," a shaky voice on the other side of the receiver announced.

Frank was my mom's best guy friend. I think he'd wanted to date her a while back, but as far as I knew, they were just friends. Close enough friends that he often came to family events, even the ones my mom wasn't hosting.

This was the first time Frank had ever called me.

"Oh, hi, Frank," I replied. "How are you?"

There was a pause.

"I've got some bad news," he finally said. "I was supposed to meet your mom for dinner tonight. We have a standing Saturday-night dinner date."

"Okay," I said, feeling my heart start to beat quickly.

"I got to her apartment around five o'clock and knocked on her door, but she didn't answer. Then I tried calling her, but she didn't pick up." He paused. "So I used the key she gave me in case of an emergency and opened the door. She was lying on the couch, Kate, and didn't look so good. I tried to wake her up, but she wouldn't move."

I could feel the tears starting to stream from my eyes.

"I'm so sorry, Kate, she's gone."

I don't remember what he said after that. But I do remember feeling weak. Almost like I was floating . . . like I was seeing the room, but not really there. I walked toward our sitter, who'd met my mom several times, and said simply, "My mom just died, I need to go."

Then I ran for the door.

‡ ‡

The next few days were a blur. The boys were too young to understand death, but they knew "Mommy is sad, and Safta isn't coming back." On the one hand, I'd been preparing for my mom's death for most of my life; on the other, I felt blindsided by her sudden departure. Part of me was heartbroken, another part relieved. The latter emotion made me feel terrible and terribly guilty.

We sat shiva at my brother's house in New Jersey the first two days, then at my and Mike's apartment in the city for the third. Jacob and Gideon didn't attend any of the planned events, but our sitter did bring them up from the playroom for the tail end of the final shiva at our home. There's nothing like two delicious almost-four-year-old twin boys to make people smile at a shiva, especially two delicious almost-four-year-old boys wearing khaki pants and polo shirts and clutching a matchbox car and naked Barbie, respectively. My mom would have loved seeing my boys mingle with the crowd, and she'd have gotten a kick out of Gid braiding the hair of one of my coworkers after our rabbi wrapped the minyan service.

‡ ‡

"Can I style your hair this morning?" G asked a few months later, about a half hour before we were set to meet Uncle Brian, Aunt Aditi, and cousins Anya and Arjun at the Liberty Science Center.

That day, Jacob and Gideon were dressed similarly—in sweatpants and T-shirts—and sported near identical haircuts. The big difference? Gideon walked through the science center, from exhibit to exhibit, clutching a Barbie.

"Mama," he whispered to me as we were waiting in line for the Mars simulator. "That kid keeps looking at me and my Barbie."

"Which kid?" I asked.

He nodded in the kid's direction.

"It doesn't seem like he's paying any attention to you or your Barbie," I said softly. "But if you see him staring, why don't you say something like, 'I see you looking at my Barbie. Do you have any questions?'"

"Mom, I'd never say something like that," Gid hissed back. "I just don't like him looking at me that way."

I explained to Gideon that while it was true that there was no such thing as a boy toy or a girl toy, it was more common to see a girl walking around holding a Barbie. And because of this, some people might stare at him. So, I told him, he had a few choices: He could walk around *not* holding the Barbie. He could walk around holding the Barbie and worry about what people said or thought. Or he could walk around holding the Barbie and not give a shit how anyone felt about it. I phrased the third option a bit differently, but that was the gist.

Gideon held on to Barbie for a few more exhibits, but when we hit the pixel-art display on the second floor, he asked me to put her in my bag.

"Are you sure, buddy?" I asked him.

"I'm sure," he said, and walked toward the wall of blinking colors looking slightly defeated.

‡ ‡

I'll admit I was glad when Gideon grabbed Yoga Barbie the following Monday as he headed for school. As much as I worried about people making fun of him, I wanted him to stay true to himself. And I smiled when I arrived in the playroom of our building that evening and saw Jacob playing with some matchbox cars and Gideon with several Barbies.

The playroom, about 2,500 square feet in all, looked like the indoor version of most suburban day care centers' backyards, and made our address a favorite among families with young kids on the Upper West Side. It also made our kids highly requested playdates in their early years. Especially during yucky weather. Nannies didn't need to keep their kids cooped up in their respective apartments or visit the Children's Museum for the third time in a week; they could call our nanny, schedule a playdate, and spend hours on end in our playroom. The kids could run, ride tricycles and Big Wheels, climb an indoor rock structure, or play inside one of several huge plastic playhouses. Sometimes they'd go to the playroom emptyhanded and use what was there to amuse themselves; other times they'd bring some arts and crafts, building blocks, or their respective toys and dolls.

Occasionally, a visiting nanny might give Gideon's Barbies an odd stare, but the playdates kept coming, and for the most part people seemed to accept that Gideon played with Barbies and occasionally wore a tutu.

"I love that you don't care what kids think about your toys," I remarked to Gideon as he was taking a bath and dipping his Little Mermaid Barbie in the water that night.

"But I do care, Mama," he said as he looked sadly into my eyes.

"Well, I'm glad you still play with them anyway," I said, trying to hold my smile . . . and trying even harder not to cry.

‡ ‡

At some point we spoke to Gideon's feelings doctor about his "gender nonconformity." She suggested reading him a book called *My Princess Boy* by Cheryl Kilodavis during one of his weekly sessions. It was a super cute story about a little boy who, like him, liked princesses and loved playing dress-up.

"He needs to know there are other boys like him," she told me and Mike. "That it's okay to like the things he likes."

We agreed. Because it *was* okay. Right?

"*My princess boy is four years old,*" she read aloud. Gideon sat in my lap and held my hand as she read; even from behind, I could see his cheeks fill out, indicating a smile.

And that made me smile.

"*He likes pretty things,*" she continued. "*Pink is his favorite color. He plays dress-up in girlie dresses; he dances like a beautiful ballerina.*"

By the last few pages, I was struggling to hold back my tears.

"*If you see a princess boy, will you laugh at him? Will you call him a name? Will you play with him? Will you like him for who he is?*"[1]

The therapist paused for just a beat.

"*Our princess boy is happy because we love him for who he is. My princess boy is your princess boy. We love our princess boy.*"

Mike and I loved our princess boy too. We just wanted to make sure he was happy. I remembered how sad he'd looked while dipping Barbie in the bath the other night. The thought made my heart ache; my breathing grew noticeably louder.

When Gideon left the room, our therapist told me about a support group downtown for parents of gender-nonconforming kids. It was run by the Ackerman Institute for the Family, one of the nation's most well-known and well-respected institutions for family therapy.

"There's a group for Gideon too," she told me, "if he ever wants to meet kids like him."

I jotted down the name, thanked her, and said I'd look into it.

‡ ‡

A couple of weeks later, when I brought Jacob to see our feelings doctor, she asked if I'd contacted the group.

"Not yet," I admitted. "But I'm definitely planning to."

"Good," she said, and then, "I'd like to read *My Princess Boy* to Jacob today. What do you think?"

"I think that's a great idea," I replied. And I meant it.

"I think it's important Jacob knows there are other boys like his brother," she told me. "That it's okay that not all boys like the things Jacob likes . . . and that it's okay that Gideon likes the things he does."

‡ ‡

A few months later, we took Giddy and one of his best girlfriends to the American Girl store for a special outing. First, a fancy lunch (including complementary mini seating and place settings for the dolls), followed by an afternoon of doll pampering at the salon, and then, the highlight of the day, shopping for new doll outfits. Gideon and his friend had "the best day ever," and G didn't seem to mind that he was the only boy in the flagship store who actually wanted to be there.

I didn't mind either. Though I did feel like people were staring at us. At Gideon, mostly, but also at me and Mike. We were the parents, of course, the ones who'd agreed to take our little boy to the place so many little girls dreamed about. Again, I felt that strange mix of pride and discomfort gnawing at my insides.

‡ ‡

We took Jacob and a friend to a separate special outing on a separate day. Stellar seats at Yankee Stadium, complete with popcorn, hot dogs, fries, cotton candy, and a killer view of A-Rod. Our J-man and his friend were in heaven.

While I enjoyed seeing both boys happy, I felt way more comfortable at Yankee Stadium than I had in the American Girl store. Growing up, I'd spent many afternoons sitting in the stands with my dad and brother.

"Do you know who Mr. October is?" I asked Jacob at his special game, trying to impress him and his buddy with my Yankees trivia.

"No idea. Who?"

"Number forty-four. Reggie Jackson. Also known as Mr. October. He was a big-time Yankees legend in the eighties. Any idea why they called him Mr. October?"

"No, why?"

"Because the World Series usually took place in early October. And no matter how Reggie played during the regular season, any time the Yankees made it to the playoffs or the series, he'd come alive, clobbering the ball and getting lots of home runs in the post-season. And since that always happened in October, the fans started calling him 'Mr. October.'"

"Well, do you know any of the guys who play for the Yankees today?" Jacob asked, clearly unimpressed with my old-school baseball knowledge.

"You got me there, bud. Other than A-Rod and Didi, I get sort of lost."

"That's okay," he told me. "I can point out all the good players to you."

Going to games with Jacob—Yankees games, Jets games, maybe a Knicks game or two thrown into the mix—was everything I'd imagined we'd do when we had twin boys.

The last place I'd ever imagined myself was the American Girl store.

But I tried to embrace Gideon's love of dolls because I remembered what it was like to feel different. It wasn't just that I'd liked sports and preferred wearing jeans to dresses as a girl. It was also that my parents had separated when I was nine years old during the late '70s, when divorce was not nearly as prevalent as today.

Several months after my dad moved out, still well before their divorce was finalized, I began washing my hands repeatedly, fearing that I was dirty and feeling compelled to check things—to make sure water faucets were turned off, for example, and that our front door was locked. By the time a therapist diagnosed me with obsessive-compulsive disorder, my hands were so raw they were bleeding. My mom would coat them with vitamin E oil at night and make me wear gloves to sleep, in the hopes the moisture would help heal my outsides.

Inside, though, I remember feeling like a freak. And the last thing I wanted as a mom was for either of my kids ever to feel that way.

5: Why Don't My Friends Know Me?

We had just celebrated the boys' sixth birthday, and all four of us were exhausted. I tucked the guys into their beds.

We'd recently redecorated their room, yet again. Bunk beds lined one wall; space-saving built-in double desks and cabinets spanned two others. Gideon needed a place for his dolls, Jacob for his baseball cards and cars. (I picked the bedding this time: blue comforters with white stars, no questions asked.)

I kissed them both on their keppies and turned toward the living room, hoping for some adult conversation and much-needed relaxation.

Gideon often confided in me around bedtime, and often I'd barely get from the bunk bed to the door before he would cry out, "Mama, can I talk to you for a little longer?"

"Let's chat in the morning," I'd usually say. If not, I'd be in their room forever.

"Can I please have a glass of water?" Jacob would then ask.

"Can you lie with me for two more minutes?" Gideon would want to know.

"Can you tell us one more Mark story?" they'd both beg.

Jacob and Gideon both obsessed over childhood stories of me and my best friend, Mark. Most of these stories involved us chasing after the garbage truck, trying to burn ants with our magnifying glasses, or building some crazy jump for our Big Wheels that left us both bruised, battered, and laughing hysterically. Mark had lived next door, and his house had been like an extension of mine, especially after the divorce.

His mom got angry at us after school one day. Mark, his younger brother, Daniel, and I had been making mud pies in their backyard and splattering them all over their garage. When she walked out the back door and saw our mess, she screamed at the top of her lungs, "Whose idea was this? This is not okay. Go to your rooms, all of you!"

To which I replied, "But I don't have a room here."

"Find one," she said firmly.

So, I did.

I had my first sleepover at Mark's house. Naturally, I stayed in the room with him and his brother. That not all parents would feel comfortable having their girls sleep over at boys' houses—and vice versa—didn't cross my mind until years later. In fact, not until my senior year of high school did we decide I should stay in Mark's younger sister's room instead of his.

As much as I wanted to walk out of our boys' room this night, I stopped and smiled when I heard Gideon call, "Mama, two more minutes, please?"

"Sure, love," I responded and climbed back up the stairs to his top bunk.

It had been a long day. A good day, but a long day. We'd just hosted a party for about thirty of the boys' friends at Billy Beez, an indoor entertainment park filled with slides, trampolines, and foam ball–shooting cannons. It was most kids' dream, most parents' nightmare.

"There's not enough Purell in the world for this place," I would tell anyone who'd listen.

Sure enough, one dad got lost driving to the park. One kid lost his parents *inside* the park. And Billy Beez lost our birthday cake order. It didn't help that our kids were born on the same day as one of their friends and during the same week as two others. It also didn't help that their collective parents were supremely more organized than we were and had generally booked venues and secured dates well before we began discussing our boys', thereby relegating our celebrations to some meaningless date two weeks or so after their actual birthdays.

The real issue, though, was that at this point our twins were near polar opposites, enjoying almost entirely different activities and liking almost nothing—NOTHING—in common. To top it off, Jacob's friends were almost exclusively boys, Gideon's girls. And now that the kids were six and becoming more outspoken, they had tons of opinions about their prospective parties.

Even decorating the party room at Billy Beez had become "a thing." After a week of back-and-forth and countless hours of debate, the kids had decided, and Billy Beez had agreed, on two themes for their *one* party room. Half the walls would be Pixar's *Planes*, the other half My Little Pony. We'd have tablecloths, plates, and cups representing both factions and, of course, individually decorated cakes for each kid.

By the time the big day arrived, both boys seemed reasonably content with our dual-themed party plan.

But as I climbed up to the top bunk, laid my head down next to G's, and shared the little space left on his favorite princess pillow, I began to feel uneasy.

"Mama," he whimpered.

"Yes, love?"

"Why don't my friends know me?"

"What do you mean, sweetie? Of course they know you."

"No, they don't," he continued. "Only Gila got me a Barbie doll."

He was right. Gila—his best friend, the girl he said he would marry one day—was the only person at his party who'd bought him a Barbie for his birthday.

"But that doesn't mean your friends don't know you," I tried to explain.

"Yes, it does," he cried.

And then I started grabbing for strings.

"Love, the thing is, most moms and dads just go out and buy birthday gifts in bulk; they don't put that much thought into it," I tried to explain. "And when a birthday comes around, they just wrap some random gift and give it!"

"But Jacob got everything he wanted," Gideon said. "His friends know what he likes."

He had a point. Jacob had received LEGOs, Pokémon cards, a baseball board game, and a few arts-and-crafts paint-your-own-piggy-bank-type gifts. He'd eaten it all up.

With few exceptions, Gideon had received the same.

"My friends should know I hate LEGOs," he said.

"But you don't hate *all* LEGOs," I said, knowing I should keep my mouth shut but wanting to make things right. "You like *some* LEGOs. You like My Little Pony LEGOs."

"Mom," he cried. "Only Gila got me a Barbie. Why didn't any of my other friends give me a Barbie?"

"Because," I suddenly wanted to say, "their parents were too scared to get you a Barbie because *your* parents didn't go out of their way to tell them that you prefer dolls, princesses, and anything else they'd buy their own daughters." *Fail. Fail. Fail.*

"Baby," I said, wiping away Gideon's tears, "why don't we look at your gifts in the morning, figure out where they were purchased, and exchange some of them for Barbies and other stuff that you do like?"

"We can do that?" he asked, sounding a bit more hopeful.

"Of course we can." I kissed his little head. "Your friends know you, my love. And they love you. Just like Daddy and I love you."

He started to relax, and I could feel the muscles in his back beginning to unclench. I thought he was about to fall asleep when he started talking again.

"Mama," he whispered.

He paused.

"Yes, love?"

"Sometimes . . ."

"Yes?"

"I wish I was a girl."

Without almost any hesitation, I said, "Gideon, my love, Mommy and Daddy will love you whether you're a boy, a girl, or a bunny rabbit."

I'm not sure how the bunny rabbit made it into the sentence. The truth is, I had never planned what I'd say when this happened. And of course I'd known this moment would happen.

Gideon fell asleep less than a minute later, and I left the boys' room, cried, opened a bottle of wine, and poured a glass somewhat equivalent to a Starbucks venti.

6: Hello, My Name Is . . .

All I wanted on this one morning in early March was to get the kids out of the apartment, walk them to school, and drop them off at their classrooms without a major meltdown or insidious incident. Yet I could tell from the moment I walked into their bedroom that I was asking too much.

"Mommy, Gideon was playing with his stupid Barbies and woke me up," Jacob screamed as I bent down to kiss him good morning.

"Did not," Gideon screamed back from the top bunk, one hand clutching Yoga Barbie, the other an unidentifiable figurine from his new Monster High collection.

"You know you did, stupid!"

"Did not, dummy head!"

"Boys, enough!" I clapped back. "Let's try to start the day off nicely. Please. It's time to hop out of bed and get dressed for school. Your breakfast will be ready in five minutes."

"You okay?" Mike asked as I hurried into the kitchen, yanked open the freezer, and pulled out some frozen waffles.

"Nope. I'm not."

"Do you want me to make breakfast and you can chill for a little while? I can take the kids to school."

"No, it's fine. I'll take them. I want to go speak to Rabbi Rebecca or Rabbi Naomi."

"About what?"

"What do you think?" I whispered, looking over my shoulder to make sure the kids weren't nearby. Mike said nothing, so I continued, "Our kid is miserable, and I want to talk to them!"

"Well, if you change your mind and want me to take them . . ."

"I won't change my mind, Michael. Unless our miserable son miraculously turns happy in the next forty-five minutes."

"I wouldn't say Gideon is miserable," Mike replied.

"You don't have to say it. Gideon already did, and that's good enough for me."

"Did he really use the word 'miserable'?"

"I'm paraphrasing. I believe his exact words were 'I wish I was dead.'"

"Yes, but he said that when I took away his iPad last night after he refused to get into his pajamas. No kid likes to be punished."

"Michael, he's said it to me too. Several times. And I'm sure there's a connection between his increased 'not listening' and the fact that he's miserable! Besides, wasn't it you who sent that email to his feelings doctor last night?"

"I was just giving her context for this afternoon's appointment."

"Whatever," I said, opening the door of the toaster to check on the waffles. "Can you please check on the kids and let them know breakfast will be ready in one minute?"

"Of course."

I scrambled to my room, trying (again) to avoid being seen by my kids, and scrolled through the email exchange. I cried when I got to the point where Mike had written, "He often says I don't love him or like him or that he wishes he was dead or never born. I'm not sure if Kate is getting this so much, but I'm getting it a lot lately. I always explain to him that I love him and like him, etc. . . . and that I always do and I always will."

I cried harder when I reread our feeling doctor's response: "I think Gideon is having a very difficult time and feels pretty bad about himself. He is grappling with some big issues for a young kid, and I think he is taking it out on you."

I was less concerned with Gideon taking his feelings out on us and more concerned that he was feeling so horrible to begin with. What six-year-old wishes they were never born? My heart broke at the mere thought.

Because I *did* remember what it was like to want to die. But I was at least ten when I began having those thoughts—four years older than Gideon was now. At the time, I didn't understand why I was washing my hands so much, why I felt everything was getting me "dirty," and why I had scary thoughts that I couldn't get out of my mind.

Like the time I was sitting in my camp's dining room the summer after my parents split. They were serving lasagna. Normally I loved lasagna; I'd take two or three servings and still want more. But this time I looked at the filling—the ricotta cheese mixed with tomato sauce and speckled spices—and I was convinced it was the inside of a dead animal. And if I touched it—or, even worse, ate it—I would get dirty, really dirty, maybe even permanently contaminated. That my bunkmates were eating the lasagna happily made no difference. I wasn't worried *they'd* get dirty—just that *I* would.

Part of me knew the lasagna wasn't a dead animal. But another part of me wasn't so sure.

"Katie, what's the matter? Not so hungry today?" my favorite counselor, Mo, asked. "Why don't you take a little bit, so you have energy for our afternoon activities."

"Umm, I'm just not in the mood for lasagna," I lied. "I'll make a peanut butter sandwich instead." But I couldn't stop thinking about the dead animal lasagna on the platter in the center of our table, and I scrubbed my hands the moment we returned to our bunk for rest hour.

Years later, I'd learn these "intrusive thoughts" were common among people experiencing OCD. But at ten, thoughts like these made me feel scared, out of control, and sad. And yes, sometimes, like I wanted to die.

I couldn't bear either of my sons feeling this way. And I needed to talk to someone. Right away. So, I quickly got dressed and whisked the kids off to school.

‡ ‡

After getting the boys to their classes, I took the elevator to the sixth floor to see if my friend Naomi, a nonpracticing rabbi who was currently serving as the school's director of community engagement, was in her office.

By the time the elevator doors opened, I was already crying. I was so frazzled I didn't even notice that the event space I needed to walk through to reach her office was filled with about forty women— mostly moms I knew, all of them sitting in folding chairs and listening to someone speak. *Oh shit*, I thought, trying to get to Naomi's office without being noticed.

"Kate!" I heard a familiar voice whisper loudly.

I waved at my friend Jane, hoping she didn't notice my eyes were red, and knocked on Naomi's door a few times.

I waited thirty seconds.

No response.

I knocked again.

Still no response.

"Kate," Jane whispered again, this time waving me over and pointing to the empty seat beside her.

I took a deep breath, walked toward the chair, and sat down.

"Who are we listening to?" I asked.

"A mother from the synagogue who wrote a book on organizing."

"Oh, great," I said.

"*Secrets of an Organized Mom*," she added.

"Better yet," I said, though what I really wanted to hear was *Secrets of a Mom Whose Six-Year-Old Son Wishes He Was Never Born*.

"She's really good," Jane whispered.

I studied the woman at the podium. She looked like she was in her mid to late forties; her thick, shoulder-length hair was clearly fresh from a professional blowout, and her outfit and jewelry befitted someone with both money and taste. I glanced down at my faded jeans and biker boots, then to my favorite in-between-seasons jacket purchased at Loehmann's, and I felt slightly inadequate.

I was part listening, part checking my phone to see if Rabbi Naomi or Rabbi Rebecca had responded to my somewhat cryptic, clearly frenzied texts from earlier that morning.

". . . because let's face it," the woman at the front of the room said, "as much as we all love seeing our kids' artwork, few of us have the space—or even the desire—to keep it all. That's why I suggest taking a picture of each picture or project your child brings home and making a book out of them at the end of the school year. You can tell your kids it's their art portfolio."

"And what do we do with the originals?" a mom from the audience called out.

"Well, except for one or two pieces each year," the professional organizer explained, "you throw them away."

"Smart," I whispered to Jane as I looked back down at my phone for about the fifteenth time in two minutes.

I glanced around the room. Most of the moms seemed transfixed. I felt jealous. I wished I had the time and energy to have actually *chosen* to listen to this woman speak. Not that I cared so much about organizing. But I sensed I'd always have more pressing issues to deal with. That thought made me sad all over again.

Ding.

Finally, I thought to myself, except that I apparently said the word out loud.

"Finally what?" Jane whispered.

"Oh, I just heard back from Rabbi Rebecca; I've been waiting for her text to say that she's here. I gotta run."

"You don't want to wait until this is over?"

Ugh. I walked in late. Now I was leaving early. Not so classy from a social etiquette perspective. I didn't want to offend the professional organizer. Or risk stares from the other moms.

I raised my hand.

"Yes, question in the back," she said, looking my way.

"Thank you," I said. "Not quite questions, per se. But two things. One, I admittedly don't make my bed every morning, though I think your argument for doing so may have made me a convert. Two, I'm all over the taking pictures of the artwork thing. And, oh, I guess there were three things—three, I am currently so unorganized as a parent that I double-booked myself for this morning and need to jet out of here. But thank you for sharing all of this information; this was awesome!"

"Thank you for coming," the organizer said with a laugh. "Glad you enjoyed it."

I picked up my work bag, grabbed my jacket, and got up to go.

"Nicely done," Jane said. "See you later!"

‡ ‡

"I hope you don't mind I'm still in my gym clothes," Rabbi Rebecca said when she opened the door to let me into her study. "I just left SoulCycle."

"I love that you're still in your gym clothes," I said with a genuine smile.

She gave me a big hug, and I sat down just as her door opened again, and Naomi joined us. "I hope I didn't miss anything," she said, reaching over to give me a hug.

"All good," I said. "I just got here. Thanks for answering my texts so quickly."

"Of course," they said in unison.

"What's going on?" Rabbi Rebecca asked. "Are you okay?"

"No," I admitted, my eyes immediately welling up with tears. "Because Gideon isn't okay."

My rabbi friends looked concerned. I knew they cared about me and my family.

"Gideon told us he wishes he'd never been born," I told them, the tears now streaming down my face uncontrollably. "He said he wants to die." I paused and looked outside the window. "My six-year-old wants to die," I repeated, turning back to them. "And it's killing me."

"Do you know why he's so upset?" Naomi asked.

I took a breath. "Probably because he wants to be a girl. Most of his best friends are girls and he dresses up as a girl at home a lot, plays with the things most girls play with."

"That doesn't mean he necessarily wants to *be* a girl," one of the rabbis said. "Is he talking to someone? Are *you* talking to someone?"

"Yes, and yes. I'm pretty sure we're funding half the therapists on the Upper West Side." I chuckled. "But he's still miserable."

"All of the time?"

"No—I mean, he loves playing with Gila. And drawing—he's an amazing artist. But he gets down a lot. Mostly at night. Like when things quiet down and he has time to think. I'm pretty sure he's depressed, but Mike doesn't think so."

I'm not sure why I went to Rebecca and Naomi, as opposed to calling my therapist. But I think sharing with them made what was happening in our family feel more real to me. Unlike my therapist, my favorite rabbis were members of my community, my friends, people I saw on a regular basis, who I could trust to keep our conversation in confidence. While I wasn't ready to tell all my friends about Gideon, I needed to acknowledge his pain—and mine—and to admit to our reality in a public yet super safe space. My rabbi friends provided that space.

I can't recall the rest of the conversation, but I remember feeling lighter when I left the building, walked to the subway, and headed to work. I knew exactly what I needed to do.

‡ ‡

It was a few days later, on a Sunday afternoon, when a number I didn't recognize popped up on my phone. Mike and I were in Tribeca with the twins, Jack (Jacob's best bud), and his parents, who'd become close friends of ours.

Our downtown adventure had started rather hellishly. Gideon had screamed and gone ballistic during the entire subway ride. If there was one place where all his anxieties seemed to coalesce, it was on the subway. The noise, the crowds, the performers, the homeless people begging—even the mere thought of these things—were often too much for Gideon to handle. This was one of those times. I'd had to hold him on the train—literally wrap my arms and legs around him—to keep him from jumping out of his seat or hurting himself.

"Are you guys visiting from out of town? Is this his first subway trip?" someone would invariably ask me as I tried to keep his flailing under control. It was similar to the way he'd flailed as a newborn, but he was bigger now, and it was exponentially more heartbreaking to witness and exponentially more difficult—physically and emotionally—to contain him now.

"Actually, we live here," I'd say. "We take the subway all the time."

"Oh," the stranger would say, bemused. They sometimes followed up with, "Can I do anything to help?"

"No, but thank you," I'd say. "We'll be okay."

I always managed to keep a calm exterior while I matter-of-factly tried to comfort my kid. But inside, I felt like I was crumbling. Was it my fault my child couldn't ride the subway without having a tantrum? Was I failing him? Was I failing as a mother? I looked around at the other children on the subway. Most sitting semi-quietly with their parents, one or two trying to climb a pole or turning around on their seat, propping themselves up on their knees and staring out the window as our express train whizzed past several stations at a time.

I clutched Gideon harder and whispered, "You're okay, my little man. We're almost there. I promise."

‡ ‡

It could take Gideon an hour or so to come back from one of these episodes; it was almost like he was having an out-of-body experience. Thankfully, this time his cooldown went relatively quickly, and he was able to join the others about fifteen minutes later for mini golf at one of the city's outdoor courses.

The kids had just putted their balls into the last hole and we were waiting for our lunch order at the on-site café when my cell phone rang out.

"Hi, this is Kate," I answered.

"Hi, Kate, this is Ben Davis from the Ackerman Institute. I got your email inquiring about the Gender and Family Project and our parent support group, and I wanted to reach out."

"Wow, thanks for getting back to me so quickly." I motioned to Mike that I'd be back in a few, and rushed outside of the café.

Ben sounded knowledgeable, and smart, and kind, and nonjudgmental. He told me he was one of the therapists and facilitators at the monthly support groups.

I wasn't expecting his call, hadn't planned for it, so I rambled on and on nervously, as I'm apt to do. When I finally let Ben get a word in, he said it sounded like the group might be helpful for us and invited Mike and me to an intake meeting. Understandably, he needed to vet people before they attended a support group. Transgender kids and adults were frequent targets of hate, violence, and discrimination. I figured the last thing anyone at Ackerman needed was for some anti-trans, crazed lunatic to wander into their safe space with an evil agenda.

At any rate, Mike and I met with him the following week, and finally, several months later (I knew I was stalling), I wound up at my first parent support group.

‡ ‡

"Hi, my name is Kate. My pronouns are she, her, hers. I'm white, Jewish, straight, cisgender. I hope I'm doing this right."

I paused and looked around at the about thirty parents in chairs loosely arranged in a circle. The place was like the LGBTQ equivalent of Alcoholics Anonymous.

It was unseasonably warm outside, and I was starting to sweat. I was smiling, though it was forced. And my heart was beating fast, like I might throw up. "I grew up in New Jersey," I continued. "And lived all around the country doing TV news before moving to New York City. I live on the Upper West Side now with my husband, Mike, who couldn't be here tonight. We have twin boys, Jacob and Gideon, who just turned seven years old. Both of them."

I paused and waited for someone to laugh. At least three people did. Cool. The crowd liked me. I always searched for affirmation during times of stress.

"What brings me here tonight is Gideon. He's been gender non-conforming for as long as I can remember. Loves pink, purple, rainbows, and glitter . . . all things princess and mermaid. He wears dresses occasionally at home, though not at school. Most of his friends are girls, and he's told us that sometimes he *wishes* he was a girl, but not that he *is* a girl."

I took a deep breath.

"All we want is for him to be happy, and we'll support him regardless. But I'm not sure what we're supposed to do. Anyway, I'm glad I'm here tonight. I'm also scared. And sad. And I guess I just want to hear what other people in our situation have to say."

"Welcome, Kate," Jean Malpass, the founder of Ackerman's Gender and Family Project, said to me. "We're glad you're here."

The meeting was scheduled for two hours. And the group filled every second of our allotted time with talk that made my head spin.

"My son plays on his school's boys' hockey team," one mom said.

"But the summer league might have different rules, and I don't know how they treat trans kids."

"My daughter has been doing a lot better in class since she socially transitioned six months ago," another dad told the group. "But lately she's been talking about hurting herself. And the other night I found a letter she'd written saying she wants to die."

"My daughter's school isn't being supportive at all," one mom said through tears. "They keep making her use the boys' bathroom, and anytime she goes in there, the boys bully her. Last week she was so scared she tried to hold it in until school ended, and she had an accident."

I found the whole event eye-opening and, if I'm being honest, sad. All I wanted for both of my kids was to have "normal," happy childhoods. And nothing in that room felt quite normal or happy to me.

"Statistically, Gideon's probably just gay," Mike had told me repeatedly. "Less than one percent of people are trans, so the odds are way against us."

Mike found comfort in numbers. I called him "spreadsheet man." He could work on spreadsheets for hours and not get bored. Our family budget had more tabs and columns than any I'd ever seen.

"Want to see something cool?" he would say at one of our monthly budget meetings, which had gradually become our "once every five months or so budget meetings" since we'd had the twins.

"Sure, what's so cool?" I'd lie, because I could imagine nothing cool about a spreadsheet. And then he'd proceed to click on some note that brought him to a formula that showed we were spending .02 percent less on paper goods than we had the year before.

"Wow, that's pretty good, right?" I'd ask.

"It is. I mean, it's not like we're going to retire on the savings, but everything adds up."

Sometimes I sipped wine during our budget meetings because it made the spreadsheets more tenable, if not comprehensible. Because the same numbers that calmed Mike unsettled and confused the hell out of me.

"Babe, statistics mean nothing," I'd tell him, "especially if you *are* the friggin' statistic! I mean, someone's got to be the one in fifty billion to come down with the rare form of cancer, or the one in seventeen million who wins the Powerball, or the one whose kid is transgender."

This notion, and my increasing belief that we were about to win the trans lottery, had prompted me—finally—to take this next step. And I left that night thinking, *These are my people.* Even though we came from different backgrounds, walks of life, and financial situations, we all shared a bond. Each of us had our own "Gideon." Some of their kids had socially transitioned at two years old, some at nine or ten. Some toggled back and forth between gender identities; some were simply gender nonconforming.

When I walked out of the center, turning onto Broadway, and headed toward the subway that first evening, I was in a fog. I hadn't left the meeting with clear-cut answers or a plan . . . but I was now pretty sure his transition wasn't a matter of if, but when.

7: The Caitlyn Jenner Effect

A few months later, in the spring of 2015, news reports confirmed the rumors: Caitlyn Marie Jenner had transitioned. The former college-football-playing, Olympic Decathlon–winning, three-time-marrying *Keeping up with the Kardashians* star had come out as a transgender woman. Her *20/20* interview with Diane Sawyer would become the most-watched TV news magazine segment ever. The *Vanity Fair* cover story that followed—complete with Annie Leibovitz photographs—garnered a record nine million online visitors in the first twenty-four hours alone.[1]

I became slightly obsessed with the media coverage. I desperately wanted to know how Caitlyn was being received—specifically, what people were saying and thinking about her and her transition. But I never read the actual magazine article or watched the ABC broadcast; I wasn't quite ready to engage with Caitlyn herself. At least not yet. Perhaps my response mirrored my own engagement with Gideon, who was, in so many ways, living a girl's life, but not *as* a girl.

The reactions to Caitlyn's very public transition, both in the media and on the street, did not surprise. The people I expected to accept Caitlyn did. Actress and activist Lena Dunham was quick to tweet, "I just want Caitlyn Jenner to take me out and teach me how to drive a stick shift in heels."[2] President Obama applauded her bravery, tweeting, "It takes courage to share your story. Your story matters in the fight for LGBT rights."[3]

The pundits at Fox News were, of course, less than supportive, one anchor declaring Jenner merely "dressed as a woman," another comparing her transition and *Vanity Fair* cover to the end of American civilization. "Rome, final days. But that's fine," Neil Cavuto said on air.[4]

For the most part, the left applauded, the right condemned. But even many accepting liberals noted the obvious advantages Caitlyn had as a wealthy, white, famous trans person and admitted that her experience was far from typical. The odds of happiness, success, longevity, and even solvency are largely stacked against the trans population. According to the National LGBTQ Task Force, transgender people are twice as likely to be unemployed and four times more likely to live in poverty compared with the general population. And as Kylar W. Broadus, director of the group's Transgender Civil Rights Project, has noted, "these disparities are much greater for transgender Black and Latina women."[5]

A study released in April 2020 called "Transgender Status, Gender and Identity and Socioeconomic Outcomes in the United States" found that transgender adults experience not only greater economic hardships but also worse health than their cisgender counterparts. They are 14 percent less likely to have completed college, and 11 percent less likely to have jobs. Christopher Carpenter, who coauthored the study, explained, "Economists call this an unexplained gap, but likely discrimination plays a role."[6]

But it wasn't the job statistics that concerned me; my kid was still six and wouldn't be sending out résumés for upwards of a decade. It was the suicide statistics that made me wince.

A study published by the American Academy of Pediatrics said that more than half of transgender male respondents had attempted suicide, and almost 30 percent of transgender females surveyed said they had tried to kill themselves.[7] And this was just teenagers.

As overwhelmed as I was becoming with all this dire information about trans lives, I was also contending with a more immediate question: *Do I tell Gideon about Caitlyn's transition?*

Truth be told, I wasn't even sure Gideon knew what transgender meant. Certainly, I had never mentioned the term to him. And for good reason: I was too scared. What if he said, "Oh, Mommy, that sounds a lot like me." I wasn't prepared to open that door.

Instead, I called my best friend, Lauren, who lived outside LA with her husband and kids.

"Did you see the cover of *Vanity Fair*?" I asked when she picked up the phone.

"Well, hello to you too!" she said, laughing.

"Oh, right! Hi, how are you? How are the kids? How's Jason?" And then, before she could answer—"So, did you see the cover of *Vanity Fair*?"

"With Caitlyn Jenner? Of course I did. The Kardashians live in my town, you know."

"They do?"

"Yup, but clearly we don't run in the same circles."

"Clearly." I laughed. "I'm debating whether to tell G about Caitlyn. What do you think? Are you telling your kids?"

"My kids are older; they already know about Caitlyn."

"Well, did Emma talk to you about it?"

Emma was Lauren's ten-year-old daughter. Her ten-year-old daughter who had recently refused to wear dresses, begun shopping in the boys' section of department stores, and started wearing her brother's hand-me-downs.

"I mean, we all talked about Caitlyn Jenner at dinner the other night, but Emma didn't react any different than Zach."

"Hmmm."

"Do *you* think you should tell Gideon?" she asked.

"I have no idea," I admitted. "That's why I'm calling you!"

‡ ‡

Later that day, I checked in with the kids' feelings doctor. I figured she had to have suggestions on how—or even if—I should talk to Gideon about Caitlyn.

"Gideon's got a lot going on right now," she said to me. "I'm not sure we need to add Caitlyn Jenner to the mix."

"I guess it might freak him out?" I suggested.

"It could," she said.

"Yeah, you're probably right," I agreed.

Over the prior several months, Gideon had begun growing visibly more anxious. We could barely leave our apartment without testing his nerves. Even the mere sight of Lulu, our neighbor's Pomeranian puppy who Gideon had played with every time we saw her in the hallway once upon a time, now provoked screaming.

And then there was school. Socially, he was thriving. He and Gila's standing playdate was the highlight of his week, and now that his speech and occupational therapies were winding down, he spent the remaining afternoons playing dress-up or drawing with his other gal pals. But academically, his teachers had just raised a red flag and were now strongly recommending we hire a reading tutor for the summer.

Part of me was annoyed. Why hadn't we been told that our kid was having any academic issues—let alone one that required us to shell out money for a tutor—until the last two weeks of kindergarten? But another part of me wasn't really surprised: Jacob was zipping through the books he brought home weekly from kindergarten. Gideon? Not so much.

But it wasn't Gideon's reading that kept me awake at night. I was much more worried about his growing list of anxieties.

"Mama," he would whisper in my ear as he peeked inside a birthday goodie bag. "If I eat this lollipop, will I get fat?"

"Of course not, love," I'd say every time. "Enjoy the lollipop!"

"The kid is six," I'd say to Mike. "What six-year-old boy is worried about his weight?"

"None that I know of," Mike admitted. "And of all people—he's a beanpole!"

That was an understatement. Gideon was the second-tallest kid in his grade, next to Jacob, and so light I could still lift him up and throw him over my head to give him shoulder rides.

Gideon grew especially anxious when we talked about going to Myrtle Beach that summer. "Mama, I don't want to go on the plane— please don't make me go on the plane," he pleaded almost a month before we were scheduled to leave.

"Why not, Gideon? We take the plane to Myrtle Beach every summer."

We spent a week there every August, renting a beachfront condo two floors above one of Mike's best friends, Axel, and his wife, Julianne.

Julianne and I appeared very different on just about every level. She was about ten years older than me, had grown up in Upstate New York in a Catholic family, and now lived down South with her husband and teenage boys and was a stay-at-home mom, while I was a Jersey-born Jew who would never dream of quitting my job; being a TV reporter–turned-producer was a huge part of my identity, and I couldn't imagine not wielding a microphone in the field to interview people or sitting in an edit bay while "crashing" to meet a deadline. But Julianne and I had clicked early on. She was down-to-earth, more so than many of Mike's friends' wives, and that was a big draw for me. She was also fun and funny. We could sit for hours over a bottle of wine, telling stories, catching each other up on our lives, and quite literally laughing out loud. We both loved pop culture, good food, a good drink, riding waves in the ocean, and rolling our eyes at our respective husbands, who seldom understood what was making us crack up.

Beyond the fun, though, we could talk, really talk. About things that mattered. I knew Julianne hadn't lived the easiest life. She'd been dealt more than her share of tough breaks and, like me, understood mental illness and the toll it could take on family. She was also honest about the challenges—even the disappointments—that came with motherhood and often confided in me about the troubles of her older son, who was having a tough time navigating both school and friendships. When my mom died, she'd been one of the first to reach out.

The best part, though, was that she was who she was and didn't seem to give a damn what other people thought. If she noticed a hot lifeguard patrolling the beach, she'd say, "Wow, biceps looking extra strong today, Mr. Lifeguard!" and not care who heard. I liked that. And I liked her.

What's more, my kids liked her. Despite the absence of a shared bloodline, Jacob and Gideon loved their "North Carolina aunt and uncle" and had called them Aunt Julianne and Uncle Axel from the moment they learned to talk. They especially looked forward to their special week together in the summer, highlighted with boogie boarding, digging in the sand for crabs, and exploring the beach. Aunt Julianne had a special way with the guys. Much like Tali, our former speech therapist, who could ease Gideon out of a tantrum with a simple gaze, Aunt Julianne's mere presence seemed to calm him.

I reminded Gideon of all these things when he told me he was scared to fly to Myrtle Beach this year.

"Aunt Julianne is so excited to see you, love!" I told him. "She and Uncle Axel would be so bummed if we didn't come this year."

"Why can't we just drive there?" he asked. "Uncle Brian and Aunt Aditi drive there with Anya and Arjun."

"You hate long car rides! Do you know how long it takes to drive to South Carolina?"

"Three hours?" he suggested.

"More like twelve," I explained. "The flight is only an hour and fifteen minutes. We'll be there before you know it."

‡ ‡

Gideon wasn't entirely convinced by my logic, but he remained largely distracted by day camp for at least the first part of the summer. It was his and Jacob's second summer of "big kid" camp. Like many city kids, they waited on a street corner a block from our apartment every morning and boarded a bus to the suburbs with a bunch of kids from the neighborhood. Forty-five minutes later, they'd step off the bus onto thirty-five acres of woodlands, rolling hills, open space, perfectly manicured ball fields, multiple pools, horse stables, even go-kart tracks. And the camp also offered enough activities like cooking and arts and crafts that we felt sure Gideon would enjoy himself there as much as Jacob would.

And he did. He especially loved playing with two girls at our bus stop and braiding the hair of several others on the way to and from camp. A handful of moms approached me on Visiting Day to compliment Gideon's hairstyling abilities.

"You should see his updo," I told one.

"Really?" she asked in a tone bordering on disbelief.

"Really," I said. "The kid's got mad skills."

The mom nodded, her expression suggesting something between admiration and confusion.

‡ ‡

A few weeks later, when we hopped off the plane in Myrtle Beach to sunny skies and temperatures in the mid-eighties, Gideon, who had survived the flight, exclaimed, "I'm so excited to see Aunt Julianne and Uncle Axel." He was literally grinning with anticipation.

"I hope they brought their dogs this time," Jacob added. "Olivia, their dogs are even cuter than yours!"

"Wow, that's saying a lot," Olivia said with a laugh. She was no longer our nanny—hadn't been for several years. She'd already earned her master's degree and was teaching special education at a school in the Bronx. But she had summers off, and we'd convinced her to come with us to help with the kids and make some extra cash to help pay for her upcoming wedding.

Within about two hours, we'd dropped our bags and headed to the beach, and were already enjoying the sun and sand.

"This is awesome," I said to Julianne as we positioned our beach chairs toward the sun and she handed me a beer.

"The weather has been incredible the past few weeks," she replied. "You guys really came at a great time."

"Honestly, I'm just happy to be here—the beach *always* makes me happy. And we were really looking forward to seeing you guys this summer."

Both statements were true. The beach has always been my safe place. As a kid on the Jersey Shore, I'd spend hours playing in the water, getting pummeled by waves, building sandcastles, and eating my favorite summer treats—Lik-M-Aid and mega-size Pixy Stix. To this day, I can't pass up a Lik-M-Aid or Pixy Stix.

"You know you're eating pure sugar?" Mike asked every time he saw me grab a pair of scissors to cut the top of the straw.

"I do, and I love it," I'd tell him, followed with an overly dramatic tilt of my head and ceremonious pour of purple sugar into my salivating mouth.

After my parents got divorced, it was my dad who took over most of the beach duties. And while he was indeed a true sun worshipper, moving his chair every hour like a human sundial, he was quick to leave his sunbathing perch and take us kids into the water whenever we asked. I didn't fully understand the significance of this until I became a parent. My kids don't care if the sun is out or the water is freezing; they want to take the plunge immediately. With my dad in mind, I almost always acquiesce, while my smiles and laughter simultaneously belie the agony.

There was a sensory component, too, I realized over the years, that added to my love for the beach. I liked the way the sand felt on my feet as I walked toward the water, the salty smell and heavier weight of the air, the way the sun warmed my skin. The same sensory elements that sent Gideon reeling when he was a toddler made me feel secure. Comfortable. At home.

I'd been planning to talk to Julianne about Gideon—his new reading tutor, our first Ackerman meeting, and that he'd brought an American Girl doll and several Barbies with us. But almost before I could get a word out, Julianne put down her beer, shook her head in disgust, and showed me the cover of the magazine she was reading.

"Can you believe this?" she said. "Bruce Jenner. Now a woman. What a crock."

My heart sank.

"What do you mean?" I asked. "I think it's cool she's finally being true to herself. Don't you think it must've taken a lot of courage for her to come out?"

"I think the whole trans thing is a sham," she said, then let out a sort of "harrumph." "You're either born a boy or a girl. Period. I don't buy this whole 'oh, my outsides don't match my insides' bullshit. The liberals are taking this way too far."

"The liberals?" I squeaked.

"Yeah, first Obama supports gay marriage . . . now everybody's talking about transgender rights."

I knew Julianne and Axel voted Republican, but I'd always figured they were socially liberal. And certainly they'd never buy into the homophobic, racist rants of Donald Trump, who'd recently announced his presidential candidacy.

Right?

"I love my Obama" was all I could think to stammer—and then, trying to change the subject, "How are your kids doing these days? Will we see them at all this week?"

Evan, her oldest, was still working odd jobs, she told me, but his girlfriend was trying to convince him to get his GED, maybe apply to the police academy. And Mason had just moved into his freshman college dorm.

Not much else registered after that; I was too busy realizing that all the camaraderie I'd been looking forward to was not going to materialize, that this moment might mark the first time I was asked, even just in my head, to make a choice. To let go of something, some-one, I had previously treasured.

For the rest of the afternoon, I managed to nod along while Julianne spoke, but mostly I watched my boys jumping the waves together and wondered what Julianne would say when she came to our condo and saw Gideon's dolls.

‡ ‡

Our cousins arrived the following day, as did the family we'd befriended the summer before. They had slightly older twin girls, and ever since their first meeting, Jacob, Gideon, Georgina, and Isabella had happily built sandcastles, swum, and cheered on their respective turtles in the daily races that transformed one of the resort's two lazy rivers into a floating racetrack as a foursome.

"Go, Turtle, go! Go, Turtle, go!"

You couldn't miss the cheers coming from the South Tower at noon every day when dozens of kids, following along on land, urged their floating rubber turtles toward the finish line.

You also couldn't miss the differences between Jacob's and Gideon's turtles. On the first morning of our trip each summer, the boys would drag us to the Activities Center, where we'd purchase, then decorate, their new turtles using the waterproof sharpies laid out for just this reason. Without fail, Jacob would decorate his turtle to represent his favorite sports team du jour—red and blue for the Giants, orange and blue for the Knicks, blue stripes for the Yanks—and name it some-thing like Eli Manning, Carmelo Anthony, or Aaron Judge.

Gideon, on the other hand, would decorate his turtle with hearts, flowers, and rainbows and name it something like Angelina, Lilly, Rose, or even, one time, Lilly Rose.

Georgina's and Isabella's turtles? If turtles wore clothes, Georgina's would have been sporting surf shorts and Isabella's a tutu. As it was, Georgina generally wore surf shorts with a rash guard to the beach, while Isabella favored floral, skirted swimsuits, sometimes with a matching hat.

Seeing the twin foursome together made me smile. And I took refuge in their friendship, especially now that I'd discovered Julianne wasn't exactly the safe haven I'd thought she would be.

‡ ‡

Mike and I had planned an adults-only dinner with Julianne and Axel the night before our flight home.

"Here's money for you and the kiddos to order in," I told Olivia as I rushed around our condo putting on my last bit of makeup, throwing on my slightly wrinkled sundress, and cursing myself for not getting a keratin treatment before this trip. "Wow," I whined, "I haven't even made it outside yet and my hair is already a hot, frizzy mess."

"You look great, Kate. I wouldn't sweat it." Olivia smiled. "When do you think you guys'll be home?"

"Not too late," I told her. "Our restaurant is just five minutes away. There's wine in the kitchen. Feel free to have some once the kids are chilling out in front of the TV."

Mike and I kissed the kids good night and rushed out the door to head to dinner, determined to have the kind of good time we'd had in previous years.

But Julianne, Axel, Mike, and I had only just ordered when Julianne looked at me, referenced Obama as "my president," said something negative about the Affordable Care Act, and rolled her eyes.

Hoping to avoid conflict, I just responded, "Yeah, I know Obamacare isn't so popular with everyone these days. But—"

"Forget popular," Julianne interrupted. "You should see what it's doing to Axel's practice."

Axel, who headed up a cardiology practice in Fayetteville, didn't utter a word; he just looked on as Julianne continued.

"And, Mike, it's not like Obama's policies are so great when it comes to Israel, which you seem to care so much about. Between that and all the social programs your wife supports—"

Which is when Mike jumped in.

"Julianne, my wife is pretty knowledgeable on this stuff. You don't have to agree with her on social programs, or anything else, but you don't have to bash her either."

"No one's bashing Kate," she said.

"I don't feel 'bashed,'" I chimed in, trying to keep the peace.

But it was too late.

"Listen, *dear*," Mike said to Julianne, with a huge and slightly sarcastic emphasis—and then he launched in.

Julianne and Mike argued back and forth for the next few minutes, allegedly about policy, until Julianne had enough. Rising and grabbing Axel by the arm to join her, she said something about an Uber and stormed away.

"What the fuck was that?" I said as we stared at the empty chairs across from us, waiting for our meals to arrive.

"She shouldn't have talked to you like that!"

"I was cool with it, you know," I protested.

"That's fine, but *I* wasn't cool with it," Mike snapped. "I feel like she's been riding you all week, and sometimes enough is enough."

"You didn't need to defend me, Mike."

"I know," he said, more gently now. "But I wanted to."

"Well . . ." I paused. "Then, thank you."

But was it actually *me* Mike was defending, I wondered? Or was it our family?

Obamacare. Israel. Social programs. Julianne sure had hit on a slew of our so-called liberal values that night. I was sort of surprised she hadn't mentioned gay marriage or Caitlyn Jenner. Then again, maybe it was what she *hadn't* said that mattered most. Maybe *that* was what Mike was defending.

8: Let Them Eat Cake

Two days after we returned from Myrtle Beach and several days before the boys started first grade, we took Jacob for a planned visit to the Hospital for Special Surgery. He was having his legs serial cast to address his tiptoe walking, which, despite our best attempts, was still an issue. While toe walking is often considered "cute," the reality is that it can lead to structural foot problems—and for an athlete like Jacob, that could be especially troublesome down the road. So, after reconsulting with his orthopedist, we opted for the casts.

In medical terms, serial casting refers to a series of three casts applied to a patient to hold and stretch certain muscles in the feet and lower legs. Each set of casts is worn for two weeks, to both increase the range of motion and to weaken the muscles so that, following casting, doctors can retrain the child's walking pattern with physical therapy.

In many ways, the casts reminded me of ski boots, which are intentionally angled forward so skiers are forced to lean downhill when they head down the mountain. But ski boots are designed more for skiing, less for walking. And as a moderately graceful skier who has ungracefully clomped my way through many ski lodges and learned to balance "just so" when air squatting in a public restroom, I can say it's pretty much paradise when I unbuckle my ski boots at the end of the day and put back on a regular pair of shoes.

But Jacob didn't get to remove his casts each evening. He wore them twenty-four hours a day, seven days a week, for six weeks straight, except for the hour or so it took the cast technician to saw off one pair and replace them with a newer, more drastically angled set. Also, unlike ski boots, these casts were not made for walking . . . at all. In fact, we had to strap special booties on the casts, complete with soles and treads, so he could walk safely. And while the casts were waterproof, the booties were not, which meant we had to unstrap the booties and lift Jacob into and out of the bath every single day for six weeks.

Initially, we removed the booties before bedtime, but after Jacob woke up in the middle of the night screaming because he had to pee, we bought him a second set of booties to wear while sleeping.

Jacob wore the casts like a champ and didn't complain when school made us come in one day before classes began to prove that he could walk up and down the steps without harming himself or those around him. And on Rosh Hashana, he proudly hobbled from the pews to the front of the sanctuary and onto the bimah when our family was given "ark honors" at family services. When we finally made it to the ark, the rabbi shook Mike's hand, kissed me on the cheek, took one look at Jacob and his tie-dyed casts, and said to us, "Wow, tough summer, huh?"

‡ ‡

Two days later, when I was taking the boys to school on the crosstown bus, Jacob needed some extra time when the doors opened to jump from the last bus step to the sidewalk, and because it was rush hour and there was a crowd waiting, he seemed to garner even more stares than he and his casts normally did.

"Mommy," Gideon whispered, tugging at me, "do you think Jacob is embarrassed?"

"No, love, I don't. Why do you ask?"

"Because everyone's looking at him," he said.

I glanced over at Jacob, who was happily clomping along, carrying his backpack, his gait largely resembling that of a young Frankenstein.

"Either he doesn't notice," I said, "or he just doesn't care." I was confident it was the latter.

We traversed the couple of blocks from the bus stop to their school, and I watched both boys walk proudly into the building and give each other a high five before going their separate ways.

"We're so lucky it's Jacob who's in casts, not Gideon," I said to Mike when I returned home after drop-off. "I don't think Gideon would be able to handle them. From a sensory perspective or any other."

"I think you're right," he agreed. "Jacob's really been a trooper."

Then my thoughts turned to Gideon, who appeared genuinely surprised that Jacob didn't mind the stares. Probably because Gideon increasingly felt people staring at him even when they weren't, and the stares directed at Gideon were, as he perceived them, much less sympathetic and much more judgmental.

‡ ‡

Casts aside, the school year began unremarkably. Gideon was thrilled that he and Gila were in the same class, Jacob was thrilled to be with Jack, and I was thrilled that our family was settling into our regular school-year routine.

The thrill wore off, however, once teachers began assigning homework.

"I can't do this, Mommy!" Gideon would whine when I walked in the door at night and found him sitting at the kitchen table staring blankly at his assignments.

"Sure, you can, bud. Let me see," I'd tell him.

But the truth was, Gideon was having a rough time keeping up with his classmates.

By mid-October his teachers suggested we find him a math tutor.

"In addition to reading?" Mike asked in near disbelief when I told him. "Don't they have a learning center at school for kids who need extra help?"

"They do," I told him. "And Gideon already gets pulled out for reading and math."

"Pulled out" was what the teachers called it when a student needed extra help and left class to work with a learning specialist. I hoped it would do the trick, but I wasn't convinced.

‡ ‡

"Sometimes I feel like we're doing the whole 'square peg, round hole' thing when it comes to school and Gideon," I said to Mike around Thanksgiving.

"What do you mean by that?" he asked.

"Seriously, Mike? Isn't it obvious? First reading. Now math. Two tutors. The learning center—he feels self-conscious every time he's pulled out. The kid loses it every night trying to do his homework. Maybe he'd do better in another school."

"For the money we're paying, I think the school could try a little harder to help Gideon, don't you?"

"I think they *are* trying, Mike. But I'm not sure they're set up to help him."

"Set up to help him?"

"Yes, set up to help him," I snapped. I could feel myself getting frustrated. "Has it ever occurred to you that Gideon might learn differently? That maybe he requires something different than his brother requires? I mean, the kids are complete opposites. Isn't it possible that the school that's good for one kid might not be the right school for the other?"

"Of course it's possible. But it's first grade. It's not like they're supposed to be learning biochemistry. I'm sure if we looked at a bell curve of all the kids his age, Gideon would be right where he needs to be."

"A bell curve?" I asked incredulously. "Who cares about a goddamn bell curve! I just care about our son."

"Katie, calm down." Mike shook his head. "I care about our son too. I just don't think anything is wrong with him."

"I'm not saying something is wrong with him," I insisted. "I'm just saying maybe he learns differently. And maybe he'd do better in a different environment."

It was like déjà vu—almost the exact same conversation we'd had when Gideon was arching his back and flailing as a toddler. And once again, I was left trying to get Mike to see my point of view, to recognize that something might be different about Gideon. Not bad. Just different.

‡ ‡

I finally convinced Mike we should call a team meeting at school before the kids left for winter break. It would be a chance for Gideon's teachers, his tutors, his learning specialists, the school's head of support services, his feelings doctor, and us to discuss his academic progress.

Mike thought it was overkill, but he acquiesced.

The teachers told us Gideon was a little slower picking up new concepts, but they weren't overly worried about him.

"He tries really hard in the learning center," the learning specialist told us, "but he does require lots of repetition. And directions with multiple steps are especially hard for him to follow. That said, he's making some decent progress."

"Gideon is a wonderful member of our community," another teacher chimed in.

"That's great," I said. "I'm just wondering if this is the community that's best for him. Maybe we should get him tested? I have several friends who've gotten their kids evaluated for learning disabilities. Maybe we should give that a go?"

"I do think there's some sort of processing issue going on," our reading tutor chimed in over the phone. She taught full time at a public school downtown yet had still managed to dial in to our meeting. I was appreciative of her efforts and couldn't help but notice she was the only one on our team to flag a potential disability, or "difference," as educators now call it.

"We're not in a position to diagnose your child," the head of our school's support services told us. "But the results of a neuropsychological evaluation could shed some light on Gideon's learning profile."

"Another expense we'd need to cover," Mike turned and said to me a bit too loudly.

"If it's gonna help our son, I'm game," I said firmly.

"I don't disagree," he admitted.

And so began our search for a neuropsychologist.

‡ ‡

By early January we'd homed in on someone we liked. She was local. She came highly recommended. And she was a "she," which was important to me and Mike, because we figured it would be important to Gideon. He liked girls more than boys, and often women more than men.

The testing process, we were told, would take a few weeks, with three to four separate sittings, each two to three hours long. We wanted Gideon to feel as comfortable as possible throughout all of it.

"How come we don't know exactly how many sessions the testing will take?" I remember asking Dr. Greene in a pre-test phone call.

"It really depends on your son," she explained. "Some kids can focus for longer than others; some need to take more frequent breaks. We want to make sure Gideon is at his best when we work together; otherwise, the results can be skewed."

"Ahh, makes sense," I said.

"And the cost for testing stays the same regardless?" Mike asked.

"It does," she confirmed. "After I'm done testing him, it'll take about a month for me to send you the written report."

I had done some research and called a few schools, and hence knew that most schools in the city specializing in learning differences required a written report from a neuropsychologist in order for a student to be considered for admission. I still wasn't 100 percent sure we were headed in that direction, but I knew we needed to be prepared.

‡ ‡

"Mommy, why can't I just go to school with Jacob?" Gideon asked the first morning we were scheduled to take him in for testing.

"Because we need to go see Dr. Greene, remember? She's gonna talk to you and play some games with you for a couple of hours. Then we'll go to school."

"A couple of hours?" he whined. "Why doesn't Jacob have to go?"

"Because you and Jacob are different kids, and he does different things."

"It's not fair!" he cried.

"Giddy, I know it doesn't feel fair. But remember, Jacob had to wear casts a few months ago and you didn't. Now he goes to physical therapy twice a week, and you don't. You each need different things, love."

"Well, why do I *need* to go to Dr. Greene?" he wanted to know.

"Good question," I said. "You know how you don't love going to the learning center or having two tutors?" I asked him.

"I hate it," he growled.

"Well, Dr. Greene is going to help us figure out some things about the way you learn, so that maybe you won't always have to go to the learning center."

"So, if I go to the doctor, I can leave the learning center and go back to my regular class?"

"We don't want to put the cart before the horse," I started to explain.

"We don't want to put the what where?" he asked.

"Honestly, Gideon, we don't know if you'll be able to stop going to the learning center, but Dr. Greene might be able to help us figure out some things."

"I still don't want to go," he repeated.

"I know, kiddo, but we're going. I'll bring you to school afterward and you can see your friends then. And remember, you have a play-date with Gila this afternoon!"

"Our apartment or hers?" he asked, sounding slightly positive for the first time all morning.

"Your choice, babe. You can decide after school when Ali picks you up."

"Fine," he said.

And we headed off to see Dr. Greene.

‡ ‡

Gideon's cooperation with the testing ultimately required the guarantee of a new My Little Pony doll—promised not by me or Mike but by Dr. Greene. That the doctor herself resorted to bribery made me feel a little better about my own parenting skills. Even then, it took her the maximum number of sessions—five—to complete the testing.

"Of *course* it took five sessions," I said to Mike.

"You know it's hard for him to stay focused sometimes," he responded.

I laughed. "I'm actually sort of surprised Dr. Greene got him to finish at all."

"Well, we were paying her to do it."

"I know, Mike, but still. We can't get the kid to sit still for three minutes, let alone three hours. I just hope she's got some answers for us."

"This test isn't designed to be a silver bullet," he reminded me for what felt like the twelve thousandth time.

"I know, I know. I just hope it lets us know how we can help him."

‡ ‡

Waiting for the test results seemed to take forever.

Trying to get the kids to agree on a seventh birthday party venue took even longer. When it was clear they'd reached an impasse, Mike and I booked an afternoon of bowling on a Sunday in early February, two weeks after their actual birth date. Jacob was happy. Gideon was not.

"I hate bowling," he complained. "You know I hate bowling."

I didn't actually think he hated bowling, just that it wasn't his favorite. But yet again, we had waited too long to plan their party, and I wanted to commit to something so we could send out the invites. I knew we weren't giving Gideon the celebration he wanted. I also wasn't sure what *that* celebration would look like. I'm not sure he did either.

Despite being exhausted, I barely slept the night before the party. I'd spent most of that day rushing around town trying to purchase party favors. I had hoped one trip to Target would suffice, but somehow I also wound up at Michael's and Party City searching for stuff I thought would appeal to the thirty-six kids scheduled to show up the following afternoon. If I couldn't give both my kids the party they wanted, I'd at least make sure they were happy with the goodie bags.

"I wouldn't stress over the favors" Mike said when he walked into the living room and saw mounds of Mad Libs, mini candies, multicolored pens, and sticker strips splayed across the carpet and me stuffing all of them into individual gift bags in assembly-line fashion. "The kids will be happy with anything."

"Too late," I replied. "Besides, everyone loves a little swag."

Mike didn't say a word, just sat down beside me and helped fill the bags.

After all Gideon's apprehension, I was relieved to see both boys smiling their way through the party. Jacob enjoyed bowling with his friends and blowing out the candles on his Star Wars cake. Gideon enjoyed hanging with his girl posse and trying to blow out the candles before the wax melted all over Cinderella.

And Mike and I were too tired to care if anyone had an opinion—we just wanted the kids to have their damn cake.

9: Cain and Abel

While Gideon's close friends embraced his affinity for Cinderella, he was quickly learning that not everyone was quite as accepting. And unlike the perceived stares he'd received in the past, the comments he was beginning to field from some kids at school who disapproved of his dolls and girl-leaning tendencies were all too real. I worried about what this could do to his self-esteem. I also worried that today's hurtful comments could lead to tomorrow's violence. Sadly, the statistics only fueled my fears.

A 2015 survey conducted by the Gay, Lesbian & Straight Education Network found that 55 percent of LGBTQ youth felt "unsafe" in schools. Even more troubling (at least to me), the study revealed LGBTQ students are 91 percent more likely to be bullied or harassed than their peers, and three times as likely to be sexually assaulted.[1]

The thought of anyone hurting either of my children was unbearable. And while rationally I understood that the leap from teasing to assaulting was huge, emotionally my instincts were to protect my kids at all costs.

But what if I couldn't?

‡ ‡

"Mama," Gideon cried when I picked him and Jacob up from after-school tennis one Wednesday evening, "I'm really upset."

"What's up, little man?" I asked, giving him a hug.

"I don't want to say," he told me.

"You sure, kiddo?"

"I'm sure," he told me.

"Well, whatever it is, just know I'm here and you can talk to me or Daddy when you're ready," I said as we walked out of school.

"Do you know what happened?" I whispered to Jacob when Gideon rushed ahead to swing on some construction scaffolding.

"Nope," he said, letting go of my hand and scurrying ahead to catch up with his brother.

‡ ‡

"Mama, can you come here?" Gideon screamed out from his bath that night.

"Be there in a sec," I yelled from the other room.

I laughed when I walked into the bathroom.

"What's so funny?" Gideon asked, looking at me. He'd fashioned his hair into a sudsy mohawk and was gripping a similarly sudsy Mermaid Barbie.

"You're just the cutest!" I replied, plopping down next to the bath. "What's up, G?"

He didn't answer, just looked down.

"You doing okay?"

He shook his head from left to right.

"Does this have something to do with what you didn't want to tell me at pickup?" I asked.

He nodded.

"You want to tell me about it, bug?" I asked.

"Not really."

"Talking about it might help," I suggested.

"I don't think so," he said.

"Why don't you give it a try?"

He sighed. Then dunked his head and his Barbie under the water.

When he resurfaced, he was ready to talk. "Some boys made fun of me at tennis today," he admitted.

"I'm so sorry, love. What happened?"

"They told me only girls play with My Little Ponies and started laughing."

"Oh, kiddo, I know it makes you sad when kids make fun of your dolls."

"The girls don't make fun of my dolls," he said. "Just the boys."

"Did I ever tell you that kids made fun of me when I was your age because I liked playing sports more than I liked playing with dolls?"

"You've told me, Mom," he said. "Like five hundred times. And this is different."

"Tell me about it," I said. "I want to understand."

"It was Jacob's fault," he said and looked down.

"What do you mean?"

"'Cause it was Jacob who told the kids that I played with My Little Ponies. Then Jacob started laughing."

"Oh, love" was all I could think to say and kissed him on the head again. "I bet that didn't make you feel so good, huh."

"No, it didn't," he agreed and dunked himself and his mermaid again.

"Daddy and I will talk to your brother, okay?" I said when he reemerged.

"Okay, Mommy," he said, and reached for a towel to dry off himself and his doll.

‡ ‡

"Jacob, what happened at tennis yesterday with your bro?" I asked him the following afternoon when he was building with LEGOs.

"Did he tell you guys?" Jacob answered.

"He told us a little," Mike said, "but we want to hear your version too."

"Mommy, Gideon's so embarrassing!" he said and threw a LEGO across the room.

"What's so embarrassing?" I asked carefully.

"I hate that Gideon plays with girl stuff!"

"Well, why do you care what he plays with, Jacob?" Mike asked.

"Because!" he said angrily.

"Because why, babe?" I asked.

"Because sometimes the boys make fun of me too! And I don't like it!"

"They make fun of *you* because Gideon likes girl stuff?" I asked.

"Yes." He started to sob. "The other day at tennis someone asked if I liked Barbie dolls 'like my brother.'"

My stomach clenched. "Oh, J, I'm sorry. What did you say?"

"I don't want to tell you," he said, shaking his head.

"You can talk to us," I assured him. "We won't get mad at you."

"Yes you will," he said.

"Come on, dude," Mike chimed in. "You can tell us. We love you!"

"I told them I hate Barbies," Jacob finally said.

"What's so bad about that?" I asked. "That's true. You don't like Barbies."

"Then I told them Gideon likes My Little Ponies even more than Barbies, and the kids started cracking up."

"Ahhh, is that when they started making fun of Gid?" I asked.

"Yes," Jacob said, crying even more. Then he looked at us, bit his lip, and punched the couch. "Why can't I just have a normal brother?"

"What do you mean by that?"

"You know what I mean, Mom! A brother who doesn't like dolls and dresses and unicorns. Is that too much to ask?"

It's too much to ask of your brother, I thought. "I'm sorry it's so tough," I told him instead.

"It's really tough," he said. Then, "Why do you guys buy him all those stupid dolls?"

"We buy him dolls for the same reason we buy you LEGOs and Star Wars toys. Because he likes them."

"Well, it's really embarrassing," he said again. "Normal brothers don't play with dolls."

"*Most* boys don't play with dolls," I said with a nod. "But some do. And your brother's one of them."

"Well, I hate it!" he said.

"I hear that," I said. "But he's your twin brother, J-man. And he's the only one you'll ever have."

"Well, I wish I didn't have one at all!" he blurted out.

I took a deep breath, then exhaled slowly. "Jacob, we may not be able to stop everyone from making fun of Gideon, but we sure hope you won't make fun of him, especially in front of other kids."

Jacob was looking right at me. He nodded ever so slightly.

"And if you see other kids making fun of him, it would be really nice if you told them to stop, you know?"

"I know," he said. "But it's hard. You don't get it. He's not *your* twin brother."

Jacob was right. But I did know what it was like to have a son like Gideon. And it was hard. Really hard.

It was also hard to have a son like Jacob, who seemed increasingly confused about his brother and was getting angrier by the day.

‡ ‡

I caught my dad and stepmom exchanging worried glances at a family dinner a few weeks later.

We'd met at an Italian place in Caldwell, New Jersey, to celebrate a birthday. My brother and his family were there, along with my stepbrother and his crew—coincidentally, they had twins just a few months older than ours. The meal seemed to be going okay, until I heard arguing at the kids' end of the table and saw Jacob dangling Gideon's Barbie precariously close to a dish of marinara sauce, threatening to dunk her head.

I hopped out of my chair, grabbed Barbie from Jacob's clutch, and firmly told the kids, "We are in a nice restaurant, and you both need to behave."

"It was his fault," Gideon screamed. "He took my Barbie!"

"It's just a stupid doll," Jacob spat back. "And I didn't even do anything."

"Enough," I said to them both. "If you can't control yourselves, we'll leave now, before they bring out the birthday cake."

"Fine," they both said at once.

"But I need my Barbie back," Gideon continued.

"Barbie will be fine with me for the rest of the meal," I told him, and I took the doll to the other end of the table, where I sat back down and took a swig of sauvignon blanc.

‡ ‡

My phone rang the moment I got to work the next morning.

"Hi, this is Kate," I said cheerfully, not bothering to look at the incoming number.

"I'm getting concerned Jacob might kill Gideon one of these days," the voice on the other end said. "They were really going at it last night."

"Good morning, Dad," I said and almost laughed out loud. But then I realized my dad wasn't trying to be funny. He was serious. "Padre, it's not like we're dealing with Cain and Abel here. And besides, Gideon is scrappy. He'd probably win a death match with Jacob."

My dad didn't respond.

"Dad," I continued, "it breaks my heart that my boys are at each other's throats half the time. But sometimes it's like that with twins. It doesn't mean they're actually gonna kill each other."

"I hope you're right," he said.

The truth is, I *was* worried about my boys. I had tried to do everything right, to be and give them everything I had never had, and yet somehow they were both deeply hurting.

The thought nearly crushed me.

‡ ‡

Shortly thereafter, we received some answers on the academic front. Mike had been right about the magic bullet. There was none. And after reading the neuropsych report several times—as well as sharing it with a close friend who was a psychologist and had administered the same types of exams before—I didn't really feel like I knew much more about Gideon's learning profile than I had before the testing.

His numbers were all over the place. He scored in the 95th percentile when it came to vocabulary yet the 10th percentile for visual-spatial reasoning; he ranked in the 88th percentile for verbal comprehension, but only the 18th in processing speed. And yet Dr. Greene could offer no specific diagnosis; her conclusions were vague.

"It took you five days to administer the test," I said to her on a phone call after reading the results. "Isn't that at least a sign he's got ADHD?"

"Unclear," she replied. "We'll definitely need to watch his attention levels moving forward, but the results don't confirm there's anything to diagnose." She did list a slew of recommendations—everything from preferential seating in the front of the classroom to "continued weekly psychotherapy to address his anxiety, frustration tolerance, and self-regulation."

I felt like I should be happy with the report, should be glad nothing was technically "wrong" with Gideon. Instead, I was disappointed. I wanted answers. I wanted to be told what to do next—how to fix this, put it behind us, something more than just "continue to monitor him."

For the first time, I became jealous of Mike and his spreadsheets, where everything lined up when you used the proper formula. I sensed that Gideon's academic performance, maybe even his life in general, would never follow a formula—that, unlike other kids, he'd never fit neatly into a column or a box.

Most of all, though, I was taken aback by what was *not* highlighted in the report's conclusion or recommendations. *Forget the processing speeds*, I thought to myself. Gideon's bigger issues were clearly gender related. I was 1,000 percent confident that most seven-year-old boys didn't look at the images in the Thematic Apperception Test and see "a girl with big lips," "a girl with lots of makeup," "a girl with a big fat butt," "a boy with nipples," and several characters who wore bows or dresses. Hell, I'm confident most *girls* didn't see those things.

Dr. Greene wrote that "focus on appearance was particularly evident in his response when presented with a blank card. Gideon articulated a scene in which a girl was going to have dinner with eight friends, and he described the dresses and hair worn by each one. For example, 'Once there was a girl with brown hair and green eyes. . . . One girl had a light blue dress, one had a light purple dress, one had a light green dress . . . the sixth had rainbows on her dress . . . and they all were wearing a pink bow in their hair.'"

I became increasingly anxious as I read and reread this section. My seven-year-old son had been presented with a blank card. Essentially an oversize, bright white index card, minus the lines. And what did my kid see? A dinner party. But not just any dinner party: one elaborate enough that each of the eight attendees—all girls, no less—were wearing dresses, many of which warranted descriptions.

"Despite this level of detail," Dr. Greene's report continued, "when asked to describe the interaction between the characters, Gideon felt at a loss. Furthermore, when presented with images in which the characters appear upset, he attributed some of their emotional states to feelings about physical appearance. For example, on one card that depicted a person leaning over, he described, 'a girl is crying, and she is upset and she is wearing shoes and she has a braid. She is leaning and crying because her hair is too long and her mom won't let her cut it and her hair is very ugly but her friends all think it looks good long but she thinks it looks good short.' In another story, Gideon began by focusing on a boy who is worried and scared while looking at a violin that he is 'scared will break.' These anxious feelings seemed to lead Gideon back to his focus on gender signifiers and physical appearance."

Now, I thought, *we're getting somewhere*. My son had major anxiety, much of it centered on gender—most likely, his own gender identity. It certainly made sense to me. Yet, the report gave short shrift to the role it might be playing in his academic development.

Dr. Greene did note the following (albeit deep in the report): "For several years Gideon has been experiencing some 'gender identity issues.' He loves dolls, dresses, braiding hair, and many things associated as 'girl things.' Most of his friends are girls; however, he is accepted by and gets along well with the boys at school. He is a natural athlete but prefers not to play sports and enjoys artistic and creative activities."

Between this description and Gideon's drawings, not to mention his inability to focus for extended periods of time, I concluded my kid likely had ADHD, and even more likely was so preoccupied with his gender that he couldn't concentrate in class. And I was positive that giving him "preferential seating" wasn't going to make the slightest difference.

But again, I said nothing. Even though I saw the elephant in the room—and didn't understand how anybody who'd spent any amount of time with Gideon could miss it—I continued waiting, avoiding, and, yes, maybe even hoping I was wrong.

10: Worried Mom, Wet Kid

We rode out the rest of the school year relatively uneventfully. The head of the elementary division, along with Gideon's team of supporters (neuropsychologist, feelings doctor, learning center instructors, etc.) recommended that we keep Gideon where he was, assuring us that he didn't need a more specialized setting, that they could address his academic needs.

I wasn't convinced.

"And you're sure he's not gonna die in second grade?" I asked at our final Team Gideon meeting of the year.

"He'll be fine," they repeated.

"I don't mean die *literally*," I clarified.

"We know what you mean, Kate," the head of support services replied. "And we think Gideon can be successful here."

I still wasn't so sure, but I acquiesced. Partly because I had other issues weighing on my mind.

‡ ‡

I was becoming increasingly worried about Jacob.

I told Mike.

I told the boys' therapist.

I told my friends.

"Jacob's having a really tough time," I said to Jack's mom, Ali, after the camp bus rolled away one sunny July morning.

"Jack mentioned something the other day," she admitted.

"What did he say?" I asked.

"Just that Jacob's been kind of fighting with some of the kids lately."

"Physically fighting?" I felt my stomach drop.

"No, more like arguing and being combative."

"He's definitely pretty angry these days," I admitted.

"About what?"

"Everything and nothing, I guess. He wishes he were better in sports. He wants his own room. He wishes his brother wouldn't leave his pink shit all over the apartment."

Ali laughed.

"It *is* pretty funny sometimes," I agreed. "But not to Jacob. The other day he snapped a head off one of Gideon's Barbies."

This time we both laughed.

"I wish my boys got along better," I admitted, my tone suddenly serious.

"I know you do. My sister and I fought like cats and dogs growing up," she offered. "It wasn't until after college that we started to get close."

"I'm scared they're never gonna be close. And Jacob is just so angry. I'm scared for him, Ali. He's so young to be carrying around so much anger."

"Maybe it's not as bad as you think."

"Tell that to Gideon's headless Barbie."

We both laughed again as we entered our building. But by the time I exited at my floor and put my key in the lock, my eyes were welling up.

I cried through my shower—and my commute—that morning.

‡ ‡

Three days later, as I sat with my editor finishing up a marketing video, my cell phone rang.

Fuck, I thought to myself when I saw the camp number pop up.

"I've got to take this," I said to my editor and walked down the hall. "Hi, this is Kate."

"Kate, it's Phil from camp. Both kids are okay, but Jacob had a problem today."

Shocking, I thought. "Oyyy," I replied. "What happened?"

"Jacob slapped a counselor in the face."

"*Oh my God*," I practically yelled. "That's awful. I'm so sorry. What happened?"

"Well, I'm happy to report that Tom handled it really well."

"Wait, Jacob slapped *Tom*? Jacob loves Tom!"

"I know," Phil agreed. "And for a nineteen-year-old college kid, Tom's reaction was pretty stellar."

"So, what happened?" I asked again.

"Tom said Jacob pushed a kid in his bunk really hard, intentionally, when they were playing soccer. So Tom told Jacob he needed to take a time-out and went to sit with him while he was cooling down. Jacob apparently started trash talking to Tom; I'm not sure exactly what he said, but Tom said it was inappropriate. When Tom asked him to stop talking that way, Jacob slapped him in the face."

"Oh my God," I said again.

"And then Jacob started crying," Phil continued, "and peed on himself."

"He peed on himself?"

"He did."

"Oh, Jesus." *My poor little man*, I thought. *He must have gotten really angry, then really scared, and then felt really ashamed.* The kid hadn't had an accident for years. He had to be hurting. I wish I could have been there to hug him and let him know everything was going to be okay.

I thanked Phil for how he and Tom had handled the situation, knowing he'd be well within his rights to kick Jacob out of camp.

"We love Jacob," Phil said. "He's an awesome kid. And we know this was out of character for him. But we can't have kids hitting counselors. Or anyone, for that matter."

"You know I agree, Phil," I told him.

"I know you do, Kate. And I'm sure we can help Jacob get past this."

"Thanks, Phil, me too, and we really appreciate your support . . . and Tom's too." I paused. "So, what happens now?"

"Well, an apology is definitely in order."

"That goes without saying," I agreed. "How about this: Mike and I will send Gideon on the bus to camp tomorrow, and I'll drive Jacob up afterward so we can both talk to you. I think Jacob needs to know how serious it is for him to have hit a counselor, but also that he has the power to make things right. And then he can apologize to Tom in person."

"Sounds like a plan, Kate. Please tell Jacob we look forward to seeing him tomorrow."

"Thanks, Phil," I said again. "And I'm sorry this happened. I'm sorry my son acted out this way."

"I'm sure it will be okay," he reassured me.

Having little confidence he was right, I hung up and immediately called Mike to relay the story.

"Babe, he was so upset he peed on himself," I said through tears. "He knew what he'd done was wrong and he peed on himself. He must have felt so ashamed of his behavior and just lost it."

"It's okay, Katie. And Jacob *will* be okay, we'll make sure of it," Mike said, trying to calm me down.

"Jacob apparently told his group leader that sometimes he can't control himself," I continued through tears, "that he gets so upset he just loses it."

I felt my sadness turn to anger.

"I knew something bad was gonna happen, Mike. I kept telling you that Jacob was in crisis, that something was *really* wrong. And no one listened to me!"

"What do you mean no one listened to you? *I* listened to you!"

"Mike, you didn't listen. His therapist didn't listen. Nobody listened. I told you I was worried about him. I told you he was in crisis. And no one heard me! You *never* hear me!" The tears were streaming down my face now. I tried to make sure no one in our shared work space could see me in the semiprivate phone booth I was currently sobbing inside of.

"I listened to you . . . and I heard you," Mike said calmly. "I just didn't agree with you."

"Well, clearly you *should* have agreed with me. Because I was right."

For all the good that did any of us.

11: You Knew Last Year,
Didn't You?

The last week of summer felt like an eternity. Most of the kids' friends were still away, so playdates were tough to arrange. The weather was also unseasonably cool and rainy, which squashed my plans to crash the pool at my parents' condo complex. And work was slower than usual, so losing myself in a script or edit wasn't happening.

"Who wants to trace a body?" I asked one morning as I grabbed a new carton of Keurig cups from our front hall closet and found a roll of brown paper left over from our last move.

"Trace a body?" Jacob asked.

"You know, we'll trace your bodies, you can color them in, and we'll put them on your wall," I explained. "It'll be a fun art project."

And a way to kill at least forty-five minutes.

"Okay!" both kids said in unison, something that almost never happened.

"Awesome! Let's do it. Super J, we'll trace you first!" I unrolled the paper and Jacob lay down. "Okay, put your arms close to your sides, but not touching, and I'll trace you."

"Wait, Mom, can I put one arm up, like I'm throwing a football?"

"Great idea, kiddo." He shifted positions and I started outlining my little guy.

Two minutes later, it was Gideon's turn. He apparently didn't want to throw a football; he kept his hands by his sides, though not touching, as I traced his body.

Our babysitter arrived a couple of minutes later and smiled when she saw both kids drawing away. When I left for work, they were so preoccupied with their self-portraits that they barely noticed me kissing them goodbye.

‡ ‡

By the time I got home, the kids had taped their traced bodies to their bedroom walls.

Jacob was clearly a quarterback; his left arm was outstretched, fingers clutching the football he'd added. He'd drawn a jersey for his shirt and a big smile on his paper face. Little man looked happy, on the wall and in real life, as he stood back to admire his work.

"This is awesome, Jacob!" I said, giving him a great big hug. Then I looked on the other wall. "Oh, wow!" I said as I stood eye to eye with Gideon's creation.

"Do you like it, Mama?" he asked as he ran into his room.

"It's amazing," I said. "Want to tell me about it?"

"Not really," he said before running back out to the living room, where he was playing with his My Little Pony figurines.

Whereas Jacob had added a football to his portrait, Gideon had transformed his body entirely. Gone were his legs, and in their place was a huge green mermaid tail, with elaborate fins drawn in. Toward the top of the portrait, he had added a wavy mane of blond hair that offset his bright blue eyes.

I stood for a couple of minutes, staring at the wall and ruminating on the portrait hanging before me.

I wondered if Gideon saw himself as a mermaid. Or maybe wished he was one?

But yet again, I remained silent, not wanting to lead or influence him—and, admittedly, afraid of this point on the horizon. Because part of me knew exactly what my son was galloping toward on his little Pinkie Pie hooves.

‡ ‡

A few days later, the kids were back in school, finally. Other than being bummed that he and Gila weren't in the same class, Gideon seemed super happy to reunite with his girls and begin his afterschool sewing class. Jacob liked his teachers and the kids in his new class and couldn't wait for soccer practice to begin. Mike and I were relieved both kids were back to their routine, and were ready to get back into our own swing of things. And for two weeks, we were living the life of Genesis—where, simply put, "it was good."

Then homework began again.

And things immediately became *not* good.

Not for Gideon. And not for me.

"Mommy, I can't do this!" he would cry every night.

I tried to help Gideon with his homework. I really did. But the truth was, I hated sitting with him and trying to help him figure out the steps that seemed simple to me and second nature to Jacob. The other truth is that I wasn't particularly good at helping him. And as much as I tried to remain even-keeled, I would feel my anxiety rising in tandem with Gideon's frustration at not being able to do the same problems his brother could do with his eyes closed.

"You realize we're paying for two tutors and a feelings doctor for Gideon every week," Mike would say about once every few nights as I watched the *Rachel Maddow Show* and he tinkered with his spreadsheets.

"I do realize that. And I will only shop at Old Navy until I die. But you do realize that we're just a month into the school year and already Gideon is flailing? I knew he'd crater in second grade."

"Kate, no one's cratering. He's just having a hard time."

"'Team Gideon' promised he wouldn't die in second grade," I said, shaking my head. "Team Gideon was full of shit."

‡ ‡

Although Mike wasn't entirely convinced Gideon was in the wrong school, he agreed to taking him to an educational consultant to explore the possibilities of sending him somewhere else.

One of the first things the consultant recommended after observing him in class was that we get an updated neuropsychological exam. If Gideon were to be considered at any of the private schools for kids with learning differences, she told us, he'd need a diagnosis. And while our first neuropsych report had given us great insight into our son's imaginary dinner parties, it had fallen short on the diagnosis front.

‡ ‡

At about this time, Gideon grew tired of wearing my old hand-me-down dresses around the apartment and asked if I would buy him one of his own.

"Of course," I told him. "What did you have in mind?"

"I want to go to the store on the corner," he told me. "The one on the way to school."

"You mean Francesca's, hon?"

He nodded.

"We can totally go there, but wouldn't you prefer buying a dress from a kids' store? I'm not sure anything there will fit you."

"No, I want to go there."

Francesca's is a chain store that carries everything from dresses to boots, jewelry to candles, all at prices just above those at TJ Maxx. It wasn't where I'd envisioned buying Gideon his first dress.

But since that was what my son wanted, I put my preferences on the back burner and took him to Francesca's on the way home from school one warm October afternoon.

Jacob had a playdate at a friend's place that day, and our sitter had called out sick that morning. The timing couldn't have been better. The dress selection, on the other hand, left much to be desired—at least, according to me.

"Gideon, you sure you don't want to go somewhere with dresses closer to your size?" I asked him, sifting through a rack of clothes that might fit my five-foot-seven-inch body but would likely dwarf that of my four-foot-seven-inch son.

"No, I like these," he replied. "And I can always wear it long."

"Okay, that's an option," I agreed and moved over to the rack he was perusing. "What about this one?" I asked, holding up a super cute charcoal-colored wrap dress.

"Too dark," he said, waving me away. "I know you like gray and black," he whispered, seeming somewhat self-conscious for the first time since we'd entered the store, "but I prefer some color." And then he pulled out a blue-patterned bohemian number that, while clearly gargantuan, was actually quite nice.

"Wow, great choice," I told him. "Let's go try it on."

"Wait, we can try it on?" he asked, his eyes lighting up. "We're allowed to do that?"

"Of course, love, how else will we know if it fits?" A ridiculous question, I realized, given that none of the clothes in the store would fit him. But I figured trying on the dress was as much a part of the process as buying it.

"Will you come with me?"

"I'd love to," I told him, and grabbed a slightly smaller version of the blue dress before we walked into the dressing room together.

I didn't ask Gideon what he was thinking or feeling at the time. But I knew exactly what I was feeling. Happy for my son because he seemed happy; relieved that fellow customers probably thought we were shopping for me; and moderately anxious, because I knew we were *not* shopping for me but rather for my fashion-forward, gender-nonconforming son, who undoubtedly knew more about hemlines and this season's trends than his mother.

I was also scared. And sad. In part because I sensed there would be more dress shopping in our future—and that even if we resolved every single learning issue, there was still a lot of "hard" looming in Gideon's cards, which was not at all the trajectory I'd been hoping to give him.

"What do you think?" I asked enthusiastically as Gideon pulled the dress over his T-shirt and jeans, twirled in the mirror, and began making gestures and posing like he was walking a runway.

"I love it," he said, grinning widely. "I know it's a little big, Momma, but I'm only gonna wear it at home."

"If you love it, Gideon, we should get it."

"Really?"

"Really," I said.

Satisfied, he pulled off the dress, handed it to me, and walked out of the dressing room, leaving me standing there with an inside-out, balled-up, size small, blue-patterned dress. My son's first real dress of his own.

‡ ‡

Gideon wore the dress for about the next week straight. He'd come home from school, throw his backpack in the corner, and throw the dress over whatever he was wearing. His playdates—almost exclusively girls—didn't bat an eye.

But Jacob did.

"Why are you wearing that stupid dress?" he asked his brother more than a few times.

"Because I like it," G said every time.

"What does Gila think?" Jacob wanted to know.

"Gila told me she'd love me even if I wore a dress every day," G said defiantly.

Dear God, I hoped that was true. Gideon and Gila's friendship continued to blossom, and while they spoke less of marriage these days, her mom had just shared the cutest story with me: Gila, who spoke Hebrew at home, had asked her mom whether she thought her and Gideon's kids would speak English or Hebrew.

"How amazing would it be if Gila and Gideon got married some-day?" Mike said to me when I relayed the story.

"It would be pretty amazing," I agreed. "But I wouldn't bet on it. Besides, they'd probably argue over who got to wear the wedding dress."

"Katie!" Mike practically screamed.

"I'm kidding, babe, I'm kidding," I repeated. Though by this point I was convinced that marriage for Gideon and Gila was about as likely as me becoming a prima ballerina.

‡ ‡

As Gideon pranced in delight around our apartment in his new dress, Mike and I searched for a new neuropsych. Fall parent-teacher conferences at our Jewish day school were fast approaching, and we let his teachers know that we'd like all members of Team Gideon present. Right or wrong, I felt like Gideon's education was being held hostage, and after six years at this school, I had a list of demands. Forget the sugarcoating; we wanted—*we needed*—truthful responses. Did Gideon belong at this school? Or would he be better off somewhere else?

"Gideon's teachers have always told us he's very compliant," I told our education consultant one day. "I'm almost offended. I'm guessing he gets it from you, Mike." I let out a little chuckle. "I mean, no one would *ever* describe *me* as compliant."

"That is true, my love. No one would ever mistake you for being compliant," Mike quipped.

I laughed.

Mike laughed.

Our consultant did not laugh.

"Actually, compliance is a wonderful trait when applying to special schools," she explained. "The admissions teams want to know that your son doesn't display behavioral issues. They're happy to address learning issues. But behavioral issues? Not so much."

"Well then, 'yay' for compliance," I agreed.

‡ ‡

We regrouped with Team Gideon six days after Donald Trump defeated Hillary Clinton in the 2016 presidential election. Along with most of New York City, I was still somewhat numb and completely petrified to know that despite losing the popular vote, a man that I literally despised would soon be the most powerful man in the world. I feared for the damage Trump's racism, elitism, narcissism, and sexism could do to our country, and, closer to home, the impact his dislike/distaste/hatred for the LGBTQ community could have on my family. Never mind that he'd declared himself a "friend to women and the LGBTQ community" following the Orlando Nightclub massacre in June 2016[1]; Trump's history of homophobic and transphobic rhetoric spoke for itself.

I'd barely slept since election night, and I walked into our team meeting feeling tired, worried, emotionally hungover, and more determined than ever to go to bat for our son. I needed answers, and I needed them now.

Ultimately, Team Gideon confirmed our suspicions: the academic gap between him and his fellow students was widening, though he continued to make steady progress in the learning center and the school was willing to keep working with him in the hopes of continuing that progress.

"We're not saying he needs to leave the school," the head of the elementary school said at one point. "We're happy to keep working with him."

"And I appreciate that you're trying to help Gideon," I said, "but our bigger question is, 'Is this school a good fit for Gideon?'—and we'd like your honest assessment."

After a pregnant pause that felt like it lasted three days, the elementary head said, "Kate, we're happy to keep Gideon here for the next few years, but no, I don't think this is the best educational fit for Gideon."

I exhaled. "Thanks for your honesty. We figured that was the case. And we're planning to apply to a few specialized schools for him for next year."

"But it's only November," Mike chimed in, "so we do expect you to continue helping Gideon make progress for the rest of this school year. And, candidly, he may not get into another school, and if that happens, we expect you'll work with him next year too. You'll recall we've been really open with you about Gideon's progress, and you counseled us to keep him here."

Everyone agreed that they'd do their best to help Gideon for as little or as long as he stayed at the school, and to support us as we looked for a better fit.

As we walked out of the conference room, the head of special services turned to me and said, "You knew last year, Kate, didn't you?"

"I did," I told her. "Though to be fair, not even our neuropsych thought Gideon should switch schools then."

"Still, I'm sorry we didn't know," she said.

"Thank you," I said. And Mike and I grabbed each other by the hand and walked home.

‡ ‡

Three weeks later, Gideon met with his new neuropsychologist. Shortly thereafter, she diagnosed him with mild dyslexia and ADHD.

"I'm actually relieved," I told Mike. "At least now we know why he's struggling at school, and can get him the help he needs."

"I completely agree," Mike said. "But I don't think we should tell Gideon."

"Tell him what?" I asked.

"That he has dyslexia and ADHD."

My eyes widened. "Why not?"

"I don't want him to feel 'less than.'"

My eyes narrowed. "Why would he feel *less than*?"

"I just don't think he needs to know," he explained.

I was incredulous. "You *do* realize we're planning to send Gideon to a school for kids with learning differences, right? And dyslexia *is* a learning difference."

"I understand that," Mike said hastily, "but I still don't think he needs to know the diagnosis. I don't want him to feel bad about himself, and I also don't want him to use dyslexia or ADHD as a crutch."

"I don't think he'll feel bad about himself or use either diagnosis as a crutch," I snapped.

"Katie, can you just go with me on this one?" he asked gently.

I didn't answer.

"Please?" he pushed. "I think it's important."

"Fine," I finally said. "I won't say anything."

"And you do know we'll find a good school for him, right? He's gonna be okay."

"I know that. I *do* know he'll be okay." And for the first time in a while, I really believed that was the case.

12: The Doll Doth Protest

The good part about receiving a diagnosis? It became much easier to select the right schools for Gideon to apply to. The bad part? Between filling out the applications, visiting all the schools, and schlepping Gideon to interviews and open houses, we forgot to save the date for the kids' birthday parties . . . yet again! We did establish, though, that this year we'd throw separate parties—one for each son, on different nights, sometime in February. And we established this because Jacob and Gideon had, for the first time, informed us that they "needed" their own parties.

We billed Jacob's party as "Hibachi and Star Wars" and made sure we had the latest *Star Wars* movie ready to roll. But by the time the big night came around, he wanted to switch to a basketball theme. I made a last-minute Party City run, and we decorated our living room with almost every paper, plastic, and cardboard basketball, net, and backboard I could find. The chaos at the restaurant paled in comparison to the chaos of walking sixteen boys the four blocks back to our apartment, but the kids chilled and zoned out once we put *Space Jam* on, a great wind-down for a near-perfect celebration.

Gideon's party had taken place a week earlier, to slightly more fanfare. He'd been wanting a spa party for months, and Mike and I dived in headfirst. We secured the Ritzy Glitzy Glamour Chicks to transform our building's third-floor party room into a "salon," complete with mani-pedi, makeup and hairstyling stations, and a "pink carpet" for the fashion show that would round out the night.

Let's just say the party generated a lot of buzz in the weeks before the big night. By this point in time, most of his pals and their parents knew Gideon preferred "girl stuff," but throwing a spa party seemed like a big statement—if not to anyone else, then at least to me.

To Jacob, the party was yet another source of resentment and embarrassment.

"I am *not* going to Gideon's stupid party," he informed us.

"You don't have to go if you don't want to," I said, "but please don't call your brother's party stupid."

"Mom, it *is* stupid. Gideon is a boy. What *boy* wants a spa party?"

"Your brother wants a spa party, and we think that's great," I said evenly. "Just like we think it's great that you want a *Star Wars* party."

"Well, it's still stupid. And I'm not going."

Gideon invited eighteen girls and two boys, both of whom gracefully declined their offers for a night of pampering. Huge props to the Ritzy Glitzy Glamour Chicks coordinator, who gracefully swallowed her surprise when I explained the party was for our son, not our daughter, as she'd assumed. She did ask if we wanted to select an alternate craft, but I assured her that Gideon and his posse would actually love decorating the leopard-print sleep masks.

Meanwhile I took my party room–decorating responsibilities seriously. From the specially ordered pink and purple tablecloths to the matching polka-dotted plates and napkins, from the bouquets of balloons to the glitter we'd scatter "as needed," and all the way down to a step-and-repeat for pictures following the fashion show, I leaned in to Gideon's dream shindig. Because if we were going to throw my boy a spa party, we were gonna do it right.

I will admit that I'd long been a professional when it came to distraction. While I was happy and proud to host this less-than-traditional party, I was also nervous. For Gideon and for our family. What would the other parents think? Would their girls continue to embrace Gideon and his beauty/princess/rainbow obsession, or would they make fun of him? What would the boys at school say? Were we meeting our son where he was, or were we setting him up for disaster?

The truth is that it was easier to worry about decorations than to wonder about Gideon's growing hair, his newfound love of skinny jeans, his increasing dislike of his penis, his inability to concentrate in school, or his recent proclamation that "sometimes I think I'm just going to turn into a girl."

If this was *Jeopardy*, I was totally taking Distractions for 200.

When the big night finally arrived? Little man was totally in his element. The smile he'd last sported as Cinderella on Halloween was back. Big time.

The hair, the makeup, the nails—Gideon and his girls ate it all up. He even felt comfortable enough that night to tell his friends that he was leaving their Jewish day school.

We'd found out that Gideon had been accepted into our first-choice school two weeks before the party; I'd cried at my desk when the head of admissions called to tell me. Full-on tears of joy. My kiddo would be going to a school where they would understand his academic needs and were not only willing but prepared to help him learn.

The party was, by every account, a success. Still, Gideon cried himself to sleep that night, saying we'd handed out the "worst party favors ever."

From where I stood, my son was taking a page out of his mom's distraction book. He had been "one of the girls" that night, but now the party he'd been looking forward to for the past several months was over. The next morning, he'd be Gideon again—a boy who liked "girl things," but still a boy. My guess is these feelings overwhelmed him much more than the little makeup bags upset him.

Our whole family was figuring out ways to distract ourselves as we waited for Gideon, who either wasn't ready to admit he felt trapped in a boy's body or didn't know how to tell us. For my part, I was still too scared to even utter the word "transgender" in front of Gideon, fearful that saying the word aloud would instantly make it so. And if that happened, we'd be "that family." Just like when I was a kid. If I had learned anything growing up, it was that no one wanted to be "that family." I knew I'd always embrace and love my kiddos unconditionally, but I wasn't so sure the world would be as kind. I remembered the stares I'd get when my mom showed up at Visiting Day or one of my softball games with a new man on her arm. I could still feel those stares forty years later. I'd hated them then; I hated thinking about them now. I just wanted to protect my family.

‡ ‡

About a month after their birthday parties, Mike was serving the kids breakfast and I was putting on my Upper West Side school drop-off uniform (black leggings, black hoodie) when I heard Mike calling me from the other room.

"Hey, babe, can you come in here for a sec?" he yelled.

"Coming!" I walked out of our bedroom brushing my hair. "What's up, guys?" I asked as I joined my three boys at the breakfast table.

"Gideon just asked me a really good question, and I thought you might want to help answer it."

"What's your question, love?"

"I asked Daddy what 'protect trans kids' meant, and he called you in," Gideon replied.

"Wow," I said, trying to buy a little time. "That's a great question, Gideon. First things first, let's start from the beginning. Where did you see something that said, 'Protect trans kids'?"

"You know West Side Kids? The store where we buy everyone's birthday gifts?"

"Of course," I said as I picked at the pancake left on his plate.

"Well," he continued, "there's a doll in the window holding a sign that says, 'Protect Trans Kids,' and I asked Daddy what it meant."

Jesus Christ, I can't believe I never noticed that sign.

"So, the doll was holding a sign that said that?" I asked, still buying time.

"Yup," Gideon said.

"Well, do you know what 'transgender' means?"

"Nope," both kids replied. Jacob had joined the conversation as well.

"Well, transgender refers to a person who feels different on the inside than their parts on their outside would suggest." Yikes, this was harder than I thought. "For example, someone born with a vagina might feel like a boy inside. Or someone born with a penis could know in their heart of hearts that they are meant to be a girl. Those people are transgender. And sometimes, they realize they need to live as the person they were meant to be." I could feel a prickle of sweat on my lower back.

"What happens then?" Jacob asked.

"Well . . ." I took a breath, exhaled. "The kid born with the penis might change his name from David to Daphne and start living her life as a girl. Daphne would be transgender. The doll holding the 'Protect Trans Kids' sign," I continued, "was a reminder that we need to be nice and kind to all kids, including transgender kids." I was trying not to stare at Gideon to gauge his reaction.

"Well, that's just weird," Jacob responded.

"Who would do that?" asked Gideon.

"It might sound weird at first," I said. "But everyone is born unique. Some people are born with brown hair, or blue eyes. Some people are tall, some are small. And some are transgender. It's just one of their qualities, one of the pieces that makes them 'them.' Actually, I think it's really brave of people to realize they are transgender and live their lives as the people they know they are meant to be."

"Yeah, whatever," Jacob said. "It still sounds weird."

And within minutes, they both left the table, brushed their teeth, and grabbed their backpacks so I could walk them to school.

‡ ‡

A half hour later, when I walked past the store on my way back home to shower, I could not believe I had missed the sign before. The window display at West Side Kids was vibrant as ever, filled top to bottom with games, books, crafts, and a slew of pennants touting phrases like, "Kindness Counts," "Love Lives Here," and "Be You!" Off to the side stood two dolls with braided hair made from yarn, both wearing simple monochromatic shirts, shorts, and high-tops. And there it was, held by the doll on the left: a small sign, no bigger than an index card, with a handwritten message that simply said, "Protect Trans Kids." If there was anything that could have made me love my independent toy store more than I already did, this was it.

"Well," I said to Mike when I walked in the door, "what say you?"

"What do you mean?" he asked.

"*What do you think I mean?* What did you think of our first trans conversation?"

I felt like I'd just had twelve lattes. Was this it? Had we crossed a divide?

"I think it went as good as it could," he said.

"I tried to put it in kid terms, you know?"

Mike nodded.

"I wonder what Gideon is thinking right now." I looked eagerly at Mike. "Do you think he's sitting in class considering whether or not he's trans?"

"I don't know," he said casually. "I guess we just wait and see."

"Which is what we've been doing for, like, six years," I snapped.

Mike just looked at me.

"I'm jumping in the shower," I said, frustrated. "I'm late for work."

‡ ‡

The next few days passed without mention of the doll. And then, like a tidal wave, the questions came rolling in.

"Mama, how does someone know if they're trans?"

"Do trans kids just decide one day they're going to dress like the opposite sex?"

"Do your friends start calling you by a different name?"

"If you were born with a penis, can you really be a girl?"

I had to hand it to the kid. He asked good questions. And thanks to my frantic emails to Ben at Ackerman—and his speedy follow-ups—I felt I was able to muddle through my responses fairly well.

The one I remember most? I was crouched down, looking into G's big beautiful blue eyes, when I told him, "Having a penis doesn't make someone a boy. Just like having a vagina doesn't make someone a girl. It's how a person feels inside that matters the most. And sometimes only that person knows who they really are. The good news is that being trans is totally okay. There's nothing to be embarrassed about. Trans people can live long, happy, healthy lives just like everybody else . . . get married, have families and great jobs, the whole deal."

Even as the words came out of my mouth, I wasn't sure I was telling the truth. I knew from my visits to Ackerman that kids whose parents accepted their transitions were much more likely to live "normal" lives than ones whose parents didn't.

But I also knew how fearful the people in my trans support groups had become in the first few months since Trump had become president. Within *two hours* of being sworn into office, all mentions of LGBTQ issues had been removed from the official White House web page.[1] Did this mean all the gains of the Obama administration—everything from the repeal of "Don't Ask, Don't Tell" to legislation protecting LGBT Americans from discrimination—would be eliminated as well?

I tried not to let myself get caught up in the what-ifs, both regarding Gideon's gender identity and the role a deranged president could have on the policies that would protect him if he transitioned. But I was finding it impossible *not* to worry.

‡ ‡

About a week later, I got a call from school.

"We noticed Gideon has been more distracted than usual," one of his teachers told me when I jumped out of an edit to take her call. "We're honestly not sure if he's hearing everything we're teaching in class, let alone understanding it."

I let out a sigh, closed my eyes, and decided just to say it.

"I should probably tell you that Gideon recently learned what 'transgender' means, and I think he could be sorting things out," I explained. "I wouldn't be surprised if he was more inattentive than usual."

"Ahh," replied the director of support services. "Thanks for sharing that with us. Is there anything we can do to help?"

"I wish I knew," I admitted. "I think all any of us can do is to continue following his lead and supporting him like we've been doing."

We chatted for a few more minutes and agreed we'd all keep each other posted. I hung up the phone, went back in with my editor, and tried to pay attention to the video we were producing. But what I was really thinking was, *No wonder G is having such a hard time at school. If I had a penis but really wanted a vagina, would I be able to pay attention in class?*

‡ ‡

Gideon and I were walking home from school. It was unseasonably warm for late March, and my son had tied his sweatshirt around his waist as we trekked the seven blocks toward our apartment. I was happy he was holding my hand and glad for this time together.

"How was your day, my love? Did you and Gila play together at lunch?"

"Yup. And she let me braid her hair too!" he replied, his bright blue eyes growing wider, a proud smile plastered across his little eight-year-old face. "My first French braid!"

"Wow, that's awesome, G," I told him. "I bet she loved it. I never came close to perfecting a French braid." *Hell, I can still barely manage a ponytail*, I thought but didn't say.

"She *did* love it!" he exclaimed and then looked away. "She told me she loved it *a lot!*"

We walked the next few minutes without saying much, swinging our arms together, occasionally flashing each other a smile. Then, two blocks from our high-rise, while waiting for the light to turn, Gideon squeezed my hand a little tighter, looked up at me, and said softly, calmly, matter-of-factly, "Mama, I think I'm a transister."

I'm sure I responded instantly, but in my mind it felt like the ground swirled away below me, my head spun upward, and my insides were caught in the funnel. Here we were, in the very moment I had prepared for—and avoided and denied and role-played and denied again.

Grabbing a hold of myself, I took a breath and crouched down so I would be at Gideon's eye level, then reached for his other hand and replied, "You mean transgender, my love?"

"Yes, transgender," he continued, seemingly unaware that his mother was silently hyperventilating. "When I was in your belly, it was a mistake. I was supposed to come out a girl."

"Oh, baby, nothing about you is a mistake," I wish I had said. But instead, in more "shock mode" vs. rational reaction, I fell back on what I'd planned to say when this moment that I'd refused to admit was coming finally arrived. "It's okay, Gideon, you can be a girl. And if you say so, then you *are* a girl. Daddy and I love you and are so proud of you, and we'll help you get through this."

To this day, I'm not quite sure what Gideon thought I meant when I said, "We'll help you get through this."

I'm not even sure *I* knew what I meant—with its implication that, as always, there would be an end point, a finish line I would work us toward, a day when whatever challenge we faced would be behind us.

What I *did* know was that, as scary as that moment was, it was also a huge relief. Our child was finally figuring out who he was, and I could only hope, if not believe, that *her* life would ultimately be better because of this.

Part Two:
Our Transition

13: Can You Keep a Secret?

"I really want to tell my parents about G," I said to Mike after taking the kids to school.

He frowned. "G just told us two days ago. Can't you at least wait until it's imminent?"

"One of our sons just told us *he's* a *she*," I countered. "It feels pretty imminent to me."

"You know what I mean. He hasn't come out yet, and we don't know when he will come out."

"I really want to tell them."

"I just don't want your dad and Carol telling their friends or the rest of our family until he actually comes out. You know your dad and Carol aren't the best at keeping secrets."

"Hon, I've hardly slept at all since G told us," I said, tears pricking my eyes. "I've been crying pretty much nonstop, and I'm sort of a wreck. If I'm going to have a real relationship with my parents, I need to let them know what's happening in my life."

No comment.

"I totally get that our kid is trans, not me, but it affects me too," I tried again. "And I need to tell them. Can't you understand that?"

Mike's face softened. "Well, when you put it that way, yes, I can."

‡ ‡

It was 8:23 a.m. when Mike left for work. I picked up the phone as soon as he shut the door behind him.

I dialed, feeling like I was about to throw up.

"Hello," my stepmom answered.

"Hey, Carol, it's me. Sorry to call so early, but I wanted to talk to you and Dad about something. Can you get him on the phone too?"

"Of course. Is everything okay?"

"It will be," I told her, and then I heard her yell to my dad to pick up the phone.

"Good morning!" he practically shouted into the receiver.

"Hey, Dad. I need to tell you guys something, but you can't tell anyone. Literally."

"Okay," he said quickly.

"I'm serious, Dad, no one!"

"Kate, we won't say a word," he said.

"Carol? You too?"

"Not a problem, Kate," she agreed.

I sighed. Then paused. And started crying. "It's Gideon," I said. "It's really happening. He told us he thinks he's trans. That it was a mistake when he was inside my belly, that he was supposed to come out a girl."

"Oh, Kate," Carol said.

"I know," I managed between sobs. "I know it's the right thing. Hell, I've known he was likely trans for years. But I'm really sad. And I feel terrible for him . . . being trans has gotta be hard, especially for an eight-year-old." I heaved a breath. "I mean, I'm happy for him that he's finally realized who he is, but I'm scared. Really scared. For him and for Jacob—it's one thing to have a twin brother who likes girl stuff. Now Jacob's gonna have a transgender sister."

More silence.

"Are you guys still there?" I asked.

"We're here," they said in unison.

"I think we'll need to bring all of the cousins to therapy to explain what's going on," Carol said.

"That might be overkill," I said. "Even for our family. But remember—"

"We won't say a word, Kate," Carol jumped in.

"I appreciate that. We're trying to follow Gideon's lead. I mean, we assume he'll transition sometime over the summer, before starting at his new school. But until Gideon decides it's time, we're not telling anyone." I paused. "Except for my therapist. You guys can tell your therapists if you want, but that's it."

"We understand," my dad said.

"Thank god we all have therapists," I said, laughing, and then I started crying again.

"What happens now?" Carol asked.

"Well, the people at Ackerman gave me the names of some local therapists specializing in gender. And we're trying to get into this special program downtown, affiliated with a university hospital."

"It sounds like you're living in the right place," my dad said.

My parents had always thought we should move to the suburbs— but I guess now that one of our children was trans, the city was sounding better and better. I knew from my trips to Ackerman and all of my online support groups that we were fortunate to be living in Manhattan, where not only were there many LGBTQ allies but there was also access to some of the greatest medical and therapeutic resources in the country, if not the world. (And that assertion's not based on purely anecdotal evidence; an interactive map of programs for gender-expansive children and adolescents generated by the Pediatric Annals confirms that availability of clinical care is, in fact, much greater on the coasts of the United States, with NYC helping to lead the way. My heart goes out to trans kids in places like Kansas, Mississippi, and Louisiana, where clinical resources can range from scarce to nonexistent.[1])

Realistically speaking, I knew access to services wouldn't be the stumbling block if we left the city, because we'd only ever considered the nearby suburbs in New Jersey and Westchester. But even there we would face challenges; I was keenly aware that if we moved, we'd need to find a progressive town where my daughter and our family would be accepted, where we'd all feel safe. And while there are many towns with impressive records when it comes to LGBTQ rights, no one could convince me that any of them would be as accepting as NYC. So, for the time being, at least, we planned to stay put.

"Did I tell you we're finally breaking through to the studio apartment next door?"

"No, you didn't," Carol said. "That's amazing."

"So now the kids will each have their own rooms." I smiled with relief. "Perfect timing."

"It sounds like you and Mike are doing all the right things, Kate," Carol said.

"We're trying," I said. "It's been really hard."

"We know it has," my dad said.

"And I'm really sad," I told them and started crying again. "I know Gideon will ultimately be better off, that she'll become 'her authentic self'—that's what they call it." I paused. "Jesus, guys, I have a daughter."

"You'll all be okay," Carol said.

"I know, but—anyway, that's all I got," I said. "Just calling to tell you you're gonna have another granddaughter."

"Your dad and I are here for you, Kate, for all of you," Carol said. "Whatever we can do, just let us know."

I hung up the phone and continued crying. Not really about Gideon, but about me. While Carol had said all the right things, my dad's silence was up for interpretation, and I felt like I had let them down. That I was their kid who still caused them the most worry, even now that I was in my forties. I knew my dad loved me. That was obvious. But I got the sense he often questioned my decisions and, in some ways, my lifestyle. How much I traveled for work. How often Mike and I hired babysitters and nannies. And until he realized my kid was trans, how we were choosing to raise our kids in the city.

"Do you *like* being a mom?" he'd asked me one time when the kids were just three or four.

"Dad, I *love* being a mom," I'd answered, almost reflexively. Because I *did* love being a mom. "Why would you ask me that?"

"No reason. Just asking."

I wasn't so sure about that. And I thought a better question would have been, did my dad enjoy seeing me as a mom? Or did my kids seem so "off" to him that he wondered how I could possibly enjoy being their mother?

To be fair, Jacob and Gideon were the most "challenging" of my dad's seven grandkids. They'd seen more therapists by age seven than the other five kids combined, and that included my brother's teenagers. My twins also fought and cried more when my parents came to visit us for an hour than my stepbrother's twins did when my parents spent the whole day with them.

Early on, I felt like my dad was judging me and my parenting skills. My kids' collective discomfort clearly made my dad uncomfortable. Sometimes when he looked at Gideon, in particular, I noticed him clenching his teeth. Like when Gideon had flailed as a newborn, when he'd tantrummed as a toddler, and, more recently, when he'd gotten frustrated braiding his doll's hair. It's almost as if my dad could tell Gideon was "different" from the day he was born. And "different" scared my dad. After his marriage to my mom failed, my dad seemed to reject *anything* different.

And yet here was Gideon.

So my dad worried. Worried that my kids would face challenges many others wouldn't, that their lives would be different—*too* different, perhaps, for them to be happy or for *me* to be happy.

For now, I prayed my dad and Carol would keep Gideon's news to themselves. But my bigger hope? That my father would learn to embrace my child's differences. And that when the time was right, he'd be proud *not* to keep his granddaughter a secret.

14: Insistent, Consistent, Persistent

"How did it go?" I asked Jacob and Gideon as we left the Ackerman Institute and turned onto Broadway.

"It was fine," Gideon said.

"I'm never going back," Jacob grumbled.

We'd just left our first support groups since Gideon told us he was a transister. There were different groups for all of us—the parent group, the group for kids who were transgender or gender nonconforming, and the sibling group. Our kids didn't care which group was which. They just didn't want to go. Even Gideon told us he had no interest in meeting people who were "like him."

We went anyway.

‡ ‡

"We're going to Ackerman," I told them that afternoon. "We'll drive there."

"I don't understand why *I* have to go to this thing," Jacob complained on the way. "I'm not the one who wants to be a girl."

"We're going as family" was all I could think to say.

Despite Jacob's complaints, which he'd been voicing nonstop since we walked out of our apartment, Jacob walked right into the sibling room without looking back. Gideon, on the other hand, stood outside of his designated room for about ten minutes, until I half carried, half dragged him in.

"Hi, Ben," I said, giving him a look that I hoped conveyed, *For the love of God, can you give me some help, please?* "This is Gideon. He wasn't thrilled about coming here tonight, but I told him you were pretty cool and that he might even have some fun here."

"Hey, Gideon," Ben said enthusiastically, then handed our son some markers and a blank name tag and led him to a table filled with three or four other kids about his age. Ben began telling Gideon about the crafts project they'd be working on that night, and then added, "Why don't you write the name you'd like us to call you on that name tag, and then we'll go around and introduce ourselves in a few minutes when everyone else gets here."

I was somewhat surprised to see Gideon using a blue marker to write his name, rather than pink or purple. Mostly, though, I was relieved that he had loosened his death grip on me, and I was able to walk out of the room.

‡ ‡

Two hours later, the four of us were back outside and walking toward the parking lot.

"What did you guys talk about in there?" I asked both kids.

No response.

I looked at Mike.

We both shrugged.

"What pronouns did you use?" Jacob asked Gideon.

"He and his," Gideon responded tentatively. "What about you?"

"He and his," Jacob blurted out. "What else would I use?"

"At least they're talking to each other," I whispered to Mike. "And I guess they've both learned about pronouns."

"What did you say your name was?" Jacob asked Gideon.

"Gideon," Gideon, who was still wearing his name sticker, replied. "What about you?"

"Well, they said we could call ourselves anything we wanted," Jacob said. "So, I said I was 'Hatred.'"

"Are you serious? Hatred?" I couldn't help but jump in. "You told everyone your name was Hatred?"

"Come here, buddy." Mike grabbed his hand, gave him a side hug, and led him toward the lot.

Gideon and I walked a few feet behind them. I could see Mike trying to comfort Jacob, though I wasn't exactly sure what they were talking about.

"Mama," Gideon said quietly. He looked around to make sure no one else was listening.

"Yes, babe?"

"I want you and Daddy to start calling me Jennifer," he said. "But only when we're at home and only when it's just us."

"Just us?" I asked.

"Yes, you, me, Daddy, and Jacob."

"We'll call you anything you want," I assured him as I bit my lip and held back tears.

We got into the car and headed home. No one said a word.

As I stared out the window, all I could think was, *These are our kids, the ones we've tried to do everything for: Jennifer and Hatred.*

‡ ‡

The two months that followed were a bit of a blur. I'd spent the past four years waiting for Gideon to tell me he was a girl. And now that we were here?

I cried.

A lot.

And then?

I cried some more.

I knew we'd love our child—our daughter—no matter what. But would the rest of the world love her? Would it accept her? Would she lose friends? Gideon was a beautiful boy; strangers sometimes told me so. But would "she" be a pretty girl? As handsome as "he" was? Would she get surgery to remove her penis? What would she look like in ten years? Hell, what would she look like next year?

My mind raced continuously—the what-ifs taking over. What if she never found love? What if she never got married? What if no one wanted to marry her? What if some evil anti-trans person tried to hurt her? And the biggest one, the one that kept me up at night: What if she transitioned and still wasn't happy?

It wasn't only the suicide rates that concerned me. A study published in the *Journal of the Endocrine Society* found two thirds of transgender teens battled depression. More than 56 percent of transgender males and 25 percent of transgender females reported a history of self-harm, like cutting.[1] Other studies painted a similarly dismal picture. Sad for anyone to read; traumatic for parents like me and Mike.

Despite the statistics, which did not seem like they were going to improve under our new administration, Mike and I found some solace knowing that trans kids who received love and support from their families fared much better than those whose families shunned them, disowned them, or tried to "change" them.[2]

To be clear, part of me was genuinely happy for Gideon. But another part of me was heartbroken. For her and the struggles I knew she'd face; for Jacob, who was fast becoming the angriest little man on the planet; for Mike, because I don't think any man can fathom how any other male on the planet, especially his own son, could possibly *not* love having a penis. And, selfishly, for me.

It might sound silly, but being a mom to twin boys was a huge part of my identity. *My boys. Our little men. Little Man J and Little Man G. My guys.* That's how I referred to them—to their faces, on Facebook, even when I thought about them.

Jacob and Gideon weren't just "our kids" or "our twins." They were our *twin boys.* And I was their mom. Their mom who loved throwing a football with them in the park, playing baseball with them in the playroom, teaching them to ride bicycles in the parking lot, and roughhousing with them in the living room.

When I bumped into friends on the subway en route to work, they always asked, "How are the boys?" When people called or texted about playdates, they usually asked if "the guys" were free. What would they say when Gideon became a girl? Would they still want to play with her?

Part of me felt silly for worrying about something as petty as playdates. Just a few weeks ago, my dear friend Sandy had placed her severely developmentally disabled eighteen-year-old daughter in a group home. The decision had been excruciating for Sandy, but she knew it was best for Rachel. Rachel was born with a rare genetic disorder, and while she grew physically, developmentally she'd stopped progressing after her six-month milestones. Rachel had never uttered a word in her life. Sandy had never felt the joy of hearing her daughter say, "I love you, Mom," let alone had the opportunity to take her on a real playdate. I sensed Sandy would have traded places with me— or at least my situation—in a heartbeat. Gideon was healthy. But I reminded myself that just because my child's situation wasn't as challenging as that of some other kids, it was still hard. For him and for all of us. And the unknowns continued to haunt me.

‡ ‡

Insistent, consistent, persistent.

If a child is truly transgender, he or she will be insistent, consistent, and persistent about his or her true gender. That's what Jean Malpas told us during our first Ackerman support group. And that's what the Human Rights Campaign explained in the "Transgender Youth" portion of its website. For all of the googling I'd done about transgender kids over the past several years, I was especially grateful that the HRC devoted a portion of its website to a section literally titled "Is my child transgender?"

"At some point," the HRC explained, "all children will engage in behavior associated with different genders—girls will play with trucks, boys will play with dolls, girls will hate wearing dresses and boys will insist on wearing them—and gender nonconforming behavior does not necessarily mean that a child is transgender. That said, sometimes it does—with some children identifying as another gender than the one they were assigned by the time they are toddlers. The general rule for determining whether a child is transgender (rather than gender nonconforming or gender variant) is if the child is consistent, insistent, and persistent about their transgender identity. In other words, if your 4-year-old son wants to wear a dress or says he wants to be a girl once or twice, he probably is not transgender; but if your child who was assigned male at birth repeatedly insists over the course of several months that she is a girl, then she is probably transgender. Naturally, there are endless variations in the ways that children express themselves, so the best option if you think your child might be transgender is to consult a gender therapist."[3]

Which is exactly what we did.

‡ ‡

"First, why don't you tell me a little about yourselves and Gideon," Dr. Elizabeth Cara said to me and Mike when we first entered her office.

Dr. Cara, our new gender therapist, was a protégé of one of the foremost gender therapists in the country, if not the world. She came highly recommended, and we liked her from the get-go. We also liked that she was a very attractive, cisgender, straight, married woman with beautiful, long hair. Maybe these were things that shouldn't have mattered. But they mattered to us. We wanted Gideon speaking to a woman who represented "the mainstream." Probably because this is what Gideon seemed to prefer and, full disclosure, because we were hoping that one day Gideon would feel part of the mainstream.

We told Dr. Cara how much we loved G and his bro. How I'd sensed he might be trans by the time he was three. How G would walk with me in our neighborhood, point to shoes as women walked past us, and scream out, "Heels, flats, heels, flats!" I told her about the time G asked why his friends didn't know him and the time he told me he wanted to pull off his penis.

Dr. Cara wanted to know about each of us too. I told her how badly we'd wanted our kids, how hard we had to work to have them, and how much we loved them.

"It's sort of ironic," I explained. "I've always considered myself the farthest thing from a girlie girl. And here I've birthed a boy who is way more feminine and fashion-savvy than I'll ever be."

Dr. Cara smiled.

I admitted that my mom had likely been bipolar; had been abused as a child; had gone on to abuse drugs, alcohol, and her body as an adult; had been married and divorced four times; and had died a few years earlier at just sixty-seven. I told Dr. Cara that despite being a shitty and ill-equipped mother, she had been the best safta ever.

"You should also probably know that I was diagnosed with obsessive-compulsive disorder in fourth grade," I volunteered next. "I was a hand washer. And I had some crazy irrational fears."

"Do you still suffer from OCD?" Dr. Cara asked.

"*Suffer* is a pretty loaded word," I replied. "I mean, I *feel* OCD stuff all the time, but I guess I've learned to live with it, if that makes sense. But . . ."

"But what?"

"But I do worry about it, Dr. Cara. Not just about the OCD, per se, but about our kids' overall psychological well-being. I've always been pretty petrified that I passed along some questionable genes, you know?" I felt myself getting teary.

"Everyone passes along questionable genes," she told me. "And there's nothing to indicate that being transgender is an inherited trait."

Dr. Cara wasn't telling me anything I hadn't already read before, but hearing her say the words aloud was a relief.

"And what about you, Mike?" she asked.

Mike spent the next few minutes recounting his childhood and adult life in a more matter-of-fact way than I'd just done, leaving me to wonder what Dr. Cara made of our dynamic as a couple and as a family unit. But I didn't ask, and she didn't offer.

We traded places with Gideon, and it was our turn for the waiting room.

I wondered what G and Dr. Cara were talking about. Was G opening up to this new therapist or being tight-lipped? Was G as nervous about today as I was?

Mike and I sat holding hands. Neither of us talked much. Occasionally I'd peer down at my watch or check work emails. I thought back to my days as a TV news reporter and all those times I sat outside the courtroom, waiting for the judge to call us back inside the chamber to render a verdict. This time there was no defendant, but I still felt like my child's life was on the line.

‡ ‡

About an hour later, G bounded into the waiting room, gave me a big hug, and handed us a picture he'd drawn of a unicorn and two fairies. Dr. Cara smiled and invited Mike and me back into her office. My palms were sweating, and the ten-yard walk seemed to stretch for a mile. Mike and I sat down, clutched hands, and waited for the verdict.

G was likely trans, she told us, and she'd be happy to work with him and us through the transition process.

I felt myself exhale and my eyes begin to water. I was both happy and petrified. Thrilled that we'd found a doctor not only who specialized in this niche field but also who we already liked and trusted . . . and who G seemed to like and trust as well. Scared because we were headed into unknown territory. Not just G. Our whole family. But at least now we had someone who could help us navigate this strange new journey, wherever it might take us.

Dr. Cara suggested we continue referring to G as Jennifer at home and start using female pronouns to describe her. But again, only at home for now, where G felt comfortable being Jennifer.

"Gideon told you that?" I asked her. "That's what he wants?"

"That's what *she* wants." Dr. Cara nodded. "At least for now."

In that moment, I realized I'd naively believed when Gideon

announced he was trans that we were nearing the "end game"—that he'd pick a new name, buy some new clothes, and start self-expressing as the girl she was meant to be, and that would be it.

Suddenly, however, it was dawning on me that we weren't crossing a finish line at all; rather, we were entering a nebulous new stage—one that would go on for as long as G needed it to.

15: Hair's the Thing

If the floodgates had opened after the first Ackerman meeting, then the days following our first visit with Dr. Cara felt like we'd been bowled over by a tsunami. The questions came fast and furious.

"So, do my friends just start calling me by a new name?" Jennifer asked.

"When can I get the operation?"

"Mama, will the operation hurt?"

"Can I still stand to pee now, or do I need to sit?"

I didn't have all of the answers, but I did try to keep the "rules" straight. As per her request, we began calling her Jennifer at home. But not when friends, extended family, or anyone else was in our apartment.

When I say "we," I am referring to Mike and me. Hatred informed all of us—multiple times, using several versions of inappropriate language—that he would never call *his brother* anything but Gideon, and that Gideon would never be a "real girl."

Turned out Jennifer wasn't our only child undergoing a major change. And as worried as we were about her, we grew even more concerned for Jacob. He was the odd man out. The one who couldn't see anything positive about his twin's transition.

Jennifer was getting what she wanted and needed. She would finally be a girl.

Mike and I were getting the chance to have a happier child. A child who felt comfortable in her own skin.

Jacob, on the other hand, felt like he wasn't getting anything in this whole deal. In his eyes, he was losing his brother. Period.

‡ ‡

We looked for a new therapist for Jacob. We wanted a guy's guy, someone to whom we hoped he'd be able to relate. We also hoped that with time, Jacob would realize he was gaining a sister and a happier twin. For now, though, he was sad, angry, and embarrassed.

"Why can't I just have a normal brother?" he'd demand.

As the weeks went on, he repeated this question with greater frequency.

"I hate my life!" he'd yell at other times.

Jacob was getting more physical too. With his friends. With us. With Jennifer. He began pushing and shoving. Sometimes even punching. And I wasn't sure I could blame him. This was a lot for an eight-year-old to handle.

My heart was breaking for all of us.

I was mourning the loss of my son. That's how the experts explained it. Only after I mourned the loss of Gideon could I truly welcome the arrival of my daughter.

But I was also mourning an idea. The idea of providing my kids a more stable upbringing than my own. I was having a hard time imagining "stability" and "transgender" in the same sentence. And despite knowing otherwise intellectually, emotionally I couldn't help but think, *Of course I birthed a trans kid. Did I really expect otherwise from my damaged self?*

I also spent a lot of time evaluating my own feelings about the transgender population, a group I admittedly hadn't thought much about until now. The only time I remembered having spent time with anyone trans had been in 1999, when, a few months before my marriage to my first husband, my best girlfriends took me to see an off-Broadway show called *I Love You, You're Perfect, Now Change* and then out to dinner at Lucky Cheng's.

Lucky Cheng's, the longest-running drag cabaret in New York City, had become a staple in the bachelorette party scene. Why women who are about to be married would find "men dressed as women" (which is how they were described) so entertaining still remains a great mystery to me. But I do remember having fun that night. I also remember feeling *very* uncomfortable when I was practically dry humped by what appeared to be a scantily dressed, heavily made-up woman with a very large penis.

At the time, I'm embarrassed to admit, I thought the waitresses at Lucky Cheng's were freaks. *Why would a man want to dress in drag and sing and dance for a bunch of drunk twenty- and thirtysomething women?* I wondered. *Gross. Is this the best job these guys could get?*

Twenty years later, I view Lucky Cheng's through a hugely different lens. I wonder how many of the performers at my bachelorette party had identified as transgender. Had most of them still had penises, or had they undergone sexual reassignment surgery? Had they enjoyed their jobs, or had they found them demeaning? Had their parents known their kids worked at Lucky Cheng's? And perhaps most importantly, what about that night made me think the performers at Lucky Cheng's were "gross" and "freaks"?

The world had viewed transgender people a lot differently in 1999 than they did today. Clearly, I had too. My guess was that many of the performers had been rejected by their biological families. And that Lucky Cheng's had given them the family they didn't have.

I was grateful my daughter wouldn't need to find another family, and I would have bet money she wouldn't end up working at Lucky Cheng's when she was old enough to get a job. But even if she chose to do so, no one would ever be able to convince me that my daughter was a freak or anything remotely resembling gross. On the contrary, she was one of the most beautiful, artistic, engaging, smart, funny, brave, and perfectly imperfect little people I knew. And her imperfections had nothing to do with her penis and everything to do with the fact that no one is perfect.

I kept these thoughts to myself, though, and we did the only thing we thought we could do: we trudged on, keeping things on the down-low. G's/Jennifer's transition news was hers to share, and she wasn't ready to make the change, or the public announcement, just yet.

But following her lead was becoming increasingly hard. Something was coming that I wouldn't be able to handle; I felt it in my nervous system. It was like seeing a three-story wave on the horizon. I couldn't sleep. I couldn't concentrate at work.

When I conveyed my fears to Mike, he would say, "Yeah, but what do you *want* to have happen?"

"Good question," I would say—but wouldn't answer.

What *did* I really want? For Jacob to feel more like Jacob, less like Hatred. For Jennifer to find peace and pick another name. And mostly, for the world to be kind to both of our kids.

Jennifer's wants were a bit more concrete: for her hair to grow really long, really fast.

‡ ‡

Now that the ball was rolling, Jennifer became increasingly obsessed with her appearance, borrowing my clips and hair ties more frequently and trying to "put up" or "pull back" whatever pieces she could.

One day, after picking Jacob up from a playdate, I rang the doorbell of our apartment—I'd forgotten my key.

Jennifer answered the door, and immediately Jacob's mood shifted. He let out a deep sigh and said, "What the fuck is he wearing?" before pushing past her and grumbling into our home.

I smiled when I looked at Jennifer but cried inside when I realized why Jacob was so upset.

Jennifer was wearing the skirt she'd recently made in her after-school sewing class, a neon green tank top she'd acquired from an old '80s costume of mine, and a pair of high-heeled boots she must've "borrowed" from my closet. She was also sporting mini pigtails and bright green eye shadow that matched the tank top.

"How do I look, Mama?" she asked, putting her hands on her hips and turning in a circle dramatically.

"Beautiful. And your hair looks adorable!"

"Thanks, Mama." She beamed. "Can you tell it's growing? When do you think it will be to my shoulders?"

"Not much longer," I assured her. "Your hair grows super fast."

Satisfied, she smiled and darted off.

‡ ‡

We were still recovering from what I'd thought was a brilliant idea. Surely, I'd thought, Jennifer would love going to my full-service adult hair salon. Lots of pretty women with long hair and cool clothes, the whole shampoo and "massage your scalp" experience, and offers for coffee or tea. What could go wrong?

My Russian-born, heterosexual, Trump-supporting "hair guy"— that's what.

As much as I thought he'd understood that G was growing out his hair and that we were simply at the salon for a slight trim/shaping, Scissorhands had other ideas.

That was the last time G went to my salon and the first time he announced he would not be cutting his hair anymore.

Still, as any pop star can tell you, the journey of growing out boy-short hair into girls' hair isn't a matter of simply ignoring it until you can make a ponytail. So now I needed a suitable salon. I asked my girlfriends for recommendations, looked online, and kept my eyes peeled for places as I walked the kids to and from school every day. But no one, Yelp included, seemed to know of a place that was "good for boys who are growing out their hair so they can be girls."

Ultimately, I started walking into random salons and trying to get a vibe. While my method was entirely unscientific, I was convinced I'd know the right salon when I felt it.

It was an early evening in late spring when I intentionally got off the subway two stops north of my usual exit so I could scope out more salons.

First I saw the pride flag in the window; then I spied the small poster in the corner saying, "Hate Doesn't Live Here." *All good signs.*

I headed to the front desk, where I introduced myself to the receptionist and then blurted out something to the effect of, "Can I ask you a strange question? I'm looking for a new hair person for my eight-year-old son, who is planning to socially transition to a girl at the end of the summer. He's growing his hair and really needs a trim, but he's petrified to get it cut because the last guy chopped too much off and he went ballistic, so I was wondering if there was someone here that you thought might be a good fit? And my kid doesn't want anyone to know he's planning to transition. That's still a secret."

Without skipping a beat, the receptionist said, "Sure, I think we can help. Let me introduce you to Luna."

Luna was exactly what I'd envisioned someone named Luna would look like. Beautiful long hair, a fabulous flowing dress, perfectly manicured eyebrows, lovely light brown skin, and a gorgeous smile. She. Was. Stunning. And also, it turned out, trans. What's more, she was happy to meet Gideon and trim his hair.

Done.

I thanked her, thanked the receptionist, and left with an appointment.

‡ ‡

The first trim a week later went off without a hitch. A little cut here, a little snip there, some nice banter with Luna, and a blowout that made G feel like it was the spa birthday party all over again.

It was settled. Luna would be our new hair chick. From this day forward, she'd style my son's hair. By the end of the summer, if all went as planned, she'd style my daughter's.

16: Hello Muddah, Hello Faddah

My husband claims I'm obsessed with three things: Wash U in St. Louis; Montclair, NJ; and Camp Sequoia. Not sure I agree "obsessed" is quite an accurate description, but I get what he's saying. I'm super proud of my alma mater and fully recognize that while it used to be an "Ivy League reject" school, I'd probably never get accepted there today; I do constantly scan real estate listings in my hometown and get strangely excited, even giddy, when I meet someone with a Montclair connection. And yes, after spending eleven summers at sleepaway camp—seven as a camper, four as a counselor—I take personal pride that the Baked by Melissa founder went to my camp, as did Christina Aguilera's first husband.

Hell, if I could figure out a way to spend my summers at sleepaway camp *today*, I'd do it in a heartbeat. So when it came time to think about sending the kids, I was chomping at the bit. "One more summer till sleepaway camp," I'd mention from time to time to get the kids used to the idea.

"I can't wait!" Jacob would say. "Can I go to Jack's camp? Or Cousin Zach's camp?"

"I'm *never* going to sleepaway camp," G would say and roll his eyes. "Ever." And then, "Why would someone want to go to camp to go to sleep?"

To which I'd reply, "Kiddo, you don't go to sleepaway camp to go to sleep. You go to sleepaway camp to make friends, try new activities, and have fun. Sleeping in a bunk with your new friends is just one part of it. Think of it like an extended sleepover!"

"Whatever," he would say.

But that would likely be *next* summer, and the more I thought about *this* summer, the more I believed the kids really needed separate camps. Jacob needed space from his soon-to-be sister. G needed a camp where he could play with girls—not just their hair—where he could grow his *own* hair, and where he could continue planning his transition.

My search for this new day camp was probably the easiest part of this transition process and took place—where else but—at work, during an edit. While my editor searched for the perfect video to complement my script on corporate social responsibility and sustainability, I searched for the perfect day camp to complement my gender-nonconforming kid.

Several phone calls and only a half dozen or so Internet clicks later, I was pretty sure I'd found a camp that fit our requirements. Groups were coed, G could be placed with three of his best gal pals, and the camp would cost about half the price of the boys' previous camp. The camp to which we'd paid a nonrefundable check, eight months earlier, to secure two spots.

There was only one option.

I called the owner of the kids' old camp to explain that G would soon be a girl. That it might be easier for G if he went somewhere new. And then, placing the ball squarely in the camp's court, I asked the owner for his thoughts. He thanked me for the information, admitted the camp wasn't prepared for G's potential transition, and sent me a refund within two days.

Two separate camps with two different bus stop locations and two very similar drop-off and pickup times. It was a logistical nightmare for two parents working full-time jobs. And it was exactly what our kids needed during this critical time.

‡ ‡

Meanwhile, Jennifer continued experimenting with her hair and clothes much more that summer. I'd often walk into our apartment after work at the end of the day to see her with a new headband or clips in her hair, sporting a new dress she would still only wear at home or one of several belly shirts she'd made on her own. This usually involved cutting up one of her many tie-dyed T-shirts and adding fringes. Somewhat cute, but slightly reminiscent of what some teenage girl with permed hair and a neon bikini would have sported at the Jersey Shore in the '80s as Van Halen blasted in the background. A couple of times I almost laughed out loud when I opened the door and saw my kid in one of these getups. But she was happy. And that was good enough for me.

‡ ‡

Also, true to New York City sleepaway camp preparation form, we spent several weekends that summer visiting various camps on "rookie days." That's when kids spend a day at a given sleepaway camp playing activities, meeting the counselors, talking to current and prospective campers, and getting a feel for the camp and its culture. Our search was, of course, complicated by one burning question: Would we be able to find a camp we liked that was both prepared for and open to accepting a transgender camper?

Campers eat, sleep, and play together around the clock. Privacy is minimal, often nonexistent. Picture an old-school Loehmann's dressing room, add beds and cubbies, and you're looking at a traditional bunk. Sure, it had gotten a little weird for me one summer when my boobs started growing before some of my bunkmates', or when my friend sprouted pubic hair when the rest of us hadn't, but for the most part, we were all in the same boat. Breasts and bush aside, we all looked pretty similar and had few qualms dressing or undressing in a crowd.

But how would my penis-bearing daughter feel changing in a

room full of vaginas, I wondered? And how would the vagina-bearing girls—and, let's be honest, *their parents*—feel about their kids changing in the same bunk as a girl with a penis? Would this not even be possible? Were we looking ahead at years of Jacob off at camp while G stayed behind with us, missing out on the fun and the friendships?

Gideon actually enjoyed tagging along on a couple of the rookie days. So much so that two separate camp directors were confused.

"You're sure he's not interested in trying camp next summer?" one asked me. "He looks like he's having a blast!"

"Gideon claims he's never going to sleepaway camp," I explained quietly after pulling her aside. "The bigger issue," I whispered, "is that Gideon isn't going to be Gideon much longer. He recently realized he's transgender and plans to socially transition at the end of this summer."

"Wow," she replied, looking at G and then back at me.

I nodded. "So we're probably going to have to look at different camps for Gideon."

"Have you guys ever dealt with trans campers?" Mike asked.

"Honestly, no," she told us. And then admitted she wasn't sure the camp would be the best place for him.

We received almost the same question the following day from one of the guys who ran the camp Jacob would ultimately attend. The difference here? He *knew* his camp would not be the place for a transgender camper.

"But you know what?" he offered. "I think I know a camp you might want to consider."

"Really?" I asked.

"Really," he said, and proceeded to tell me about a nearby camp, run by the Reconstructionist Jewish movement and directed by a friend of his.

I made a mental note.

‡ ‡

I knew that camps like this existed. Because the previous summer, two weeks before sleepaway camp was scheduled to start, Lauren's then eleven-year-old had turned to her and said, "Can you please call the camp and tell them I'm now Jack and that I'll be staying in the boys' bunk?"

Lauren had obliged. As had the camp. But that was "two-week" sleepaway camp. On the West Coast. A whole different gestalt, I was learning, from the two-month camp culture of the Catskills.

Unlike G's declaration to me that she was trans, Jack's had taken Lauren by surprise. Until then, Lauren had believed her child was likely gay, maybe gender-fluid, but "definitely not trans." Despite her shock, she and her husband embraced Jared (the name Jack ultimately landed on) and his new gender identity with open arms.

Now that my kiddo was on the verge of socially transitioning, Lauren and I joked that there must have been something in the water of our off-campus apartment junior year.

"What are the odds?" I'd asked when I shared G's secret with Lauren a few months earlier.

"Seriously, Kate, I feel like we should call Maloney."

Maloney had been our landlord. At the time, we'd peppered him with questions and complaints about low water pressure, poor working heat, and fuses that burned out almost daily. Twenty years later, we joked that we should ask about the rate of transgender kids born to previous tenants.

‡ ‡

One evening that summer, G and I stood on the sidewalk outside our favorite local dinner spot waiting for his friend Amelia and her mom to arrive. As soon as the kids spotted each other, their faces lit up, they ran toward each other full speed, and they hugged for what felt like five minutes, her hand getting caught up in his now noticeably longer hair and striped sleeveless hoodie.

The hoodie was a go-to staple in G's wardrobe that summer. The top hadn't started out sleeveless; he'd cut them off a few weeks before and now rotated several plain white T-shirts that he wore under it, paired with long, baggy gym shorts, whenever he left our home. Kind of like a pre-transition uniform.

I loved watching G hang with his girls. They genuinely seemed to love him. And not just when he was styling their hair or making them special lanyard bracelets. They liked talking with him, playing with him, simply being around him.

I prayed they would also like being around "her."

Amelia untangled herself from G's hood, the kids clasped hands, and we all walked inside.

As the kids inhaled their Tater Tots and mac and cheese, I sipped cabernet and caught up with Amelia's mom, who I didn't know super well but liked very much.

"How's your summer going?" she asked.

"Pretty good," I lied. *Actually, Gideon now goes by the name Elisa. I've been doing lots of online shopping for girls' clothes and working with a contractor to break through our living room so our son and soon-to-be daughter can have their own rooms before they kill each other.*

I felt like a fraud, like I was being disingenuous by not telling her how my summer was really going. But everything centered around G's transition, and that was G's story to tell. And even though he was currently entwined with one of his best friends, he'd chosen to arrive here in boy clothes, using the name Gideon; clearly, he wasn't ready to tell it. So, like most of my "nights out" that summer, I muddled through the evening, trying to hold up my end of the conversation and wondering if anyone suspected anything was "off."

‡ ‡

An hour and a half later, we hugged our friends goodbye and wished each other a good rest of the summer. G and his gal pal swayed back and forth, her hand getting caught in G's hoodie for the second time that evening, before we parted ways.

"It looked like you guys had a great time at dinner," I said as we walked the few blocks home along Broadway.

"We did." He nodded. "But . . ."

"But what, G?"

"She told me my hair looked longer."

"It's gotten much longer," I agreed.

"But I need it to grow *really* long."

"It will, G. It will."

I knew I was telling the truth. G's hair *was* growing longer. At least an inch a month, I estimated. Who could ask for more than that?

Exactly.

‡ ‡

I began researching wigs. Real ones. Not the Rapunzel ones; the expensive ones. But how would they stay on? It's one thing for a middle-aged woman with some modicum of self-control to keep her wig intact, but I couldn't see any universe in which our cartwheel-loving, flip-in-the-pool, never-met-a-Jo-Jo-bow-he-didn't-love kid would be able to pull off wearing a wig without literally pulling the damn thing off.

One night after dinner, G threw down his brush, removed three hair clips, and flopped on the couch, muttering, "It's never gonna be long enough."

That's when my husband looked up from his computer and wondered out loud, "What about extensions?"

G's eyes lit up and he instantaneously responded, "I want extensions. Definitely extensions. Then I could be a girl."

Mike and I looked at each other and smiled.

‡ ‡

We were fast approaching a not-so-arbitrary deadline: school was set to start in six weeks, and there was no way we were going to let *his* hair delay *her* transition. New school, new gender. We felt it would be easier to make both changes at once. Dr. Cara agreed. Better to start school as a girl rather than begin as a boy and make the change in three months or so, when her hair "brushed her shoulders" or whatever benchmark or standard she selected.

We collectively decided that G would practice being a girl after camp, before school, and while on the vacation in between. Then I called Luna.

"You'd better talk to Mocha," she suggested. "She's much better with extensions."

Which is how Gideon and I found ourselves back at the hair salon discussing different options for extensions—first with Mocha and then with Traffic. Apparently, Mocha had mastered temporary extensions, but when it came to semipermanent ones (meaning those that managed to stay in for three months or more), Traffic was our better option.

"And the hair will look real?" I asked firmly.

"It *is* real hair," he told us both.

"And you've actually done this technique before?" I pressed. Instead of Mother of the Bride, I was basically now Mother of the Hair Extensions, and I was going to micromanage this until it came out perfectly.

"Absolutely," Traffic responded.

"Great," I said. "We're going to Myrtle Beach in a week and a half. Can we put in the extensions before we leave?"

"Will he be swimming in Myrtle Beach?" Traffic asked.

And the wind blew right out of my sail.

The extensions would have to wait. As much as Mike and I were willing to invest in three months' worth of hair that would help G to feel comfortable coming out, we were not willing to pay for hair that would get destroyed during a week of boogie boarding, swimming, sunshine, salt, and sand. An adult with extensions might be able to hack it, but I didn't want my fun-and-sun-loving kid to worry about hurting her hair the whole trip. We'd have to manage Myrtle Beach with G's own hair.

‡ ‡

A few nights before camp ended, my friend Viv texted me a picture of G. She must have been scouring the camp website for pictures of her daughter when she noticed it.

> *Viv: Did you see this yet?*
> *Me: No, thanks so much for sending!*
> *Viv: Gideon looks gorgeous!*

I took a closer look. G did look gorgeous.

He was sitting atop a horse, wearing a black riding helmet, his hair brushing his face and *almost* his shoulders. He was smiling, though his happiness seemed slightly tempered. I wondered what was going on in that beautiful head of his.

I texted Viv one more time.

> *Me: Wow, this might be my fave pic of the summer. Thx again!!! Xo*

I put down the phone and walked over to the kids' room to watch them sleep.

"My god, they're so beautiful," I whispered out loud.

And then I started crying, and sat on the floor and stared at them.

I still couldn't understand it. To me, J and G were perfect. Mike and I would literally say, "We have the perfect kids for us." But the more I looked at them lying under their covers—so little and so innocent—the more nothing about this process felt perfect. G hated his body; J hated having a "brother" who was so different. And I hated that my perfectly imperfect little people felt such pain. Mostly, though, I hated that I couldn't fix it.

17: Coming Out in the Carolinas

You would have thought we were packing for a nine-month trip to the tropics with all the planning behind that year's jaunt to Myrtle Beach. The online orders from Justice and Old Navy were taking over our living room; my trips back and forth to the shoe store to buy and return sandals took up most of my time outside of work.

G still wouldn't purchase girls' clothes in person, or wear them outside of our home, but between our collective cyber shopping and my frequent treks to seemingly every brick-and-mortar store selling sassy ensembles, G was gradually amassing a pretty impressive girl's wardrobe.

"How about you wear one of your new dresses to the park this afternoon?" I suggested one Sunday.

"No way, Mom," G screamed at me. "I can't do that!"

"Well, you're planning to do it pretty soon, my love. I just thought it might be fun to try now."

I looked at the growing piles of clothes on the desk she and Jacob shared.

"You like your new clothes, don't you?"

"Of course, Mommy, I love my new clothes. But . . ." G looked away. "I can't wear them outside yet. I just can't." She flopped on her bed and began to cry.

"It's okay, you don't have to wear them right now," I said softly, rubbing her little back.

"I want to." G sniffled. "But I'm too scared."

"Scared of what?"

"That people will look at me funny—or laugh at me," she cried. "My hair isn't long enough yet. Everyone will know I'm still a boy."

I didn't know what to say, so I just continued rubbing her back. I didn't tell G that I was scared too. Not just about possible negative reactions when she did finally socially transition, but also about what would happen if she wasn't ready to transition by the time school started. I couldn't imagine being stuck in this limbo any longer. The closer we came to the end of summer, the more I feared G wouldn't transition "on time." She *needed* to be a girl when she started school. *I* needed her to be a girl when she started school. Which meant I also needed to make sure she was ready.

We decided G would give the "girl thing" a go when we got to South Carolina. Mildly ironic, even scary, given the bathroom bills that had been dominating the news cycles in both Carolinas. The North Carolina legislature had passed a sweeping law in March of 2016 that reversed a Charlotte ordinance allowing people to use the bathroom that reflected their gender identity. Officially called the Public Facilities Privacy and Security Act, or HB2, the bill had overturned the protections of the Charlotte ordinance and required people to use the bathroom corresponding to their "biological sex."[1] Which meant the same transgender woman who had previously used the women's restroom would—by law—now be required to use the men's room.

For months, North Carolina had been in the national headlines as supporters and protesters held dueling rallies. LGBTQ activists argued against the bill, saying it was nothing more than a thinly veiled attempt at discrimination. Supporters of the bill, often spewing vitriol and hate, said it was simply about protecting women and children. This, despite there being literally *no statistics* reinforcing the claim that transgender women needing to relieve themselves posed a risk to cisgender women needing to pee. But this fact didn't seem to bother the bill's supporters.

The cosponsor of HB2, then Republican state representative Dan Bishop, had slammed Charlotte's initial ordinance as a "radical transgender proposal."[2] In a press release supporting his new bill, he'd written, "A small group of far-out progressives should not presume to decide for us all that a cross-dresser's liberty to express his gender nonconformity trumps the right of women and girls to peace of mind . . ."[3]

The religious right had weighed in too. "I'm not concerned about political correctness," Bishop Patrick Wooden of the Upper Room Church of God in Christ in Raleigh had said at one highly publicized rally. "Everybody knows that a transgendered woman is a man. And everybody knows that a transgendered man is a woman. And we have allowed common sense to go out of the window in the name of political correctness."[4]

The debate had droned on for about a year, until, in 2017, as part of a compromise between the Democratic governor and Republican-controlled legislature, portions of the measure were repealed. South Carolina residents had monitored the controversy throughout, with some calling on lawmakers to pass a bathroom bill in their state. Republican Governor Henry McMaster had said he saw no need to restrict restroom access for transgender people in South Carolina. But in my protective view, the damage was already done, and I feared that bringing G to Myrtle Beach would unwittingly place our kid smack dab in the middle of a transphobic firestorm.

‡ ‡

Thankfully, G was blind to the controversy and wasn't worried about where she'd pee once she became a girl; she was just scared to leave our apartment *dressed* as one.

"I'm terrified," G told me again a few days before our flight.

"I can imagine it's pretty scary," I'd say. "But Mommy and Daddy will be with you, and I promise it will be okay." Not that I could promise G that anything about being transgender would be okay.

G had already been practicing being a girl at her weekly appointments with the gender therapist: we would literally bring a bag full of her girls' clothing with us to Dr. Cara's office, and then Dr. Cara and I would leave the office so G could put on the pink leggings and bedazzled T-shirt, floral sundress, or cutoffs and cold-shoulder top we'd brought with us.

"How do you feel?" Dr. Cara asked once G was dressed and we were all back in her room the first time we did this.

"Okay." G hesitated. "Maybe a little weird."

"That's understandable," Dr. Cara said. "Why don't we walk around and introduce you to some of my coworkers?"

And with that, they began to walk the halls outside of Dr. Cara's office, yet very much *inside* the walls separating them from the bustling waiting room and Park Avenue seven floors below.

"Why don't you say hi to Rose?" Dr. Cara suggested to G when they reached one of the administrative assistants on the floor.

"Hi, Rose," G said.

"You can tell her your name," Dr. Cara prompted.

"I'm Arianna," G mumbled shyly.

"Nice to meet you, Arianna," Rose said. "Thanks for coming by to say hello!"

And that's how G practiced—though, depending on the week, G might use a different name.

So, yes, I was hoping—actually, I was *praying*—that this repeated practice would pay off when we got to Myrtle Beach. That by then, G would be able to walk off the plane in South Carolina, throw on a sundress, and sashay through our vacation with a huge smile and some extra pep in her step.

Best of all? It would happen in the company of a supportive crowd. Not only were we vacationing with her aunt Aditi, uncle Brian, and cousins, who were perhaps the most loving and accepting people on the planet, we were also meeting up with our family friends from DC, the ones with twin girls a year older than ours.

Georgina's hair had become progressively shorter and spikier each summer, and we weren't surprised to learn shortly before our trip to Myrtle Beach that she was now officially George and had socially transitioned to being a boy a few months before. *Surely*, I thought, *George's transition will put G at ease, and maybe knowing she's got a friend who understands will even make hers a little easier.*

And I would have another mom familiar with this experience to talk to, which I knew would be helpful. I still felt like I was suspended in the moment when you see the oncoming headlights. But I couldn't even articulate what the crash would be. That G would transition and not be accepted? That she would lose the friends she'd had? That she would somehow end up even more distressed than she was now? That there would be no happy ending for her? Not now, not ever? I thought about it all the time. EVERY SECOND OF EVERY DAY. *If G could just transition already*, I'd think, *then we'd be there, dealing with it, figuring it out.* It was the anticipation that was killing me.

So, yes, I was pushing South Carolina. And I was hoping that G's excitement about wearing all of her new sundresses, sandals, tankinis, and cover-ups would help move the dial. The fact that Georgina was now George? Surely that would give G the added boost she needed.

But even though G was "mistaken" for a girl as soon as we arrived at the resort, the dresses wouldn't leave our beachfront condo all week.

‡ ‡

"I see you've got a tomboy on your hands," a middle-aged blond woman said to me moments after we arrived at the resort lobby.

I looked at G—clad in baggy shorts and white T-shirt, and now with almost chin-length locks—and realized that she was indeed beginning to look more like a girl. It wasn't just the clothes; it was the whole demeanor, almost as if G's outsides were starting to resemble her insides.

And as much as I still bristled at the term "tomboy," let alone the inappropriateness of a stranger branding my kid as anything, this was the first time anyone we didn't know had verbally referred to my G as a girl. And that felt good.

‡ ‡

One morning just a couple of days into our trip, I woke up early, grabbed my laptop, and logged on to Facebook.

"I hate Facebook," my husband used to say to everyone who would listen.

"I know you do, babe," I'd answer and roll my eyes.

"And the only thing I hate more than Facebook—"

"Are the people who use it!" I'd finish for him.

"Exactly!"

"But *I* use Facebook," I'd part whine, part shout, part laugh.

"Well, okay," he'd concede. "I love you, but I still hate Facebook."

The routine never got old.

And for many reasons, I did love Facebook. It drew me closer to people, made me feel more connected. To old friends, new friends, former classmates. And now to parents, like me, who had gender-non-conforming and/or transgender kids. Sharing the joy a mom felt for her AFAB (assigned female at birth) son who'd just had top surgery and was now posing in his recovery room with a big thumbs up and a bigger smile. And also sharing the despair of a father who'd just lost his transgender daughter to suicide.

I'd been reading the message boards and posts more frequently in the past few months. I wasn't sure I'd ever post anything myself, but I knew that I felt much less alone knowing there were other parents like me, with kids like mine, out there.

But this morning I wasn't reading about chest binders, bottom surgeries, or T shots. I was looking for "likes." And I got them. The

sheer number I'd racked up for this summer's first Myrtle Beach picture made me very happy. But it was some of the comments that really
made my heart sing.

I'd posted one pic of the kids leaning over our balcony, staring
ahead at the ocean, which was only about thirty-five yards from us.
I'm sure I'd taken and posted some variation of this picture every
summer, but this year's rendition was different: Jacob, looking tan and
significantly taller than his eight years would suggest, was wearing
long basketball shorts and a LeBron jersey, his hair cut super short.
G, dark hair brushing her shoulders, stood to his left in a fitted white
T-shirt, the turquoise sweatshirt we'd bought in the girls' section of
Old Navy wrapped around her waist, concealing her gym shorts.

"Twinning in our happy place" was how I captioned the picture.

One comment stood out. "A million things I love about this picture," one of my dearest friends from college had written just a few
minutes before.

I wasn't sure if she was still online, but I instant messaged her
anyway:

*Me: Hey, babe! How are you and your gorgeous crew? I'm sure it's
not super surprising from the pics . . . but looks like G will transition to
a girl before school. Been years in the making and it's looking like the
time is now(ish)!*

*Her: I think, as I always have, that she is beautiful and looks happy.
And I think you're the best mom. I'd like to do a photo shoot with just
you and her together.*

Me: I can't wait. Thank you, Jodi!

Her: She going to change her name?

*Me: We're like on name 10. Still only in private though. Liv was
yesterday's. Today we are back to G* 😊.

*Her: Well, I hope she picks something strong and brave and full of
life like she is. Love you all!*

Me: Back at you, babe!

I wondered what my other 1,221 Facebook friends could tell from my posts. Was it obvious one of my kids was about to transition?

Was it obvious I was holding in the biggest secret of my life?

Suddenly, I realized that G might not be coming out in Carolina . . . but I was.

18: Bye, Felicia!

We arrived home from Myrtle Beach to a pile of mail, a slew of back-to-school catalogs, and two bar/bat mitzvah invitations. "We're gonna need to get G some fancy dresses," I said to Mike as I opened the invites. "And some outfits for the Jewish holidays too."

Rosh Hashana and Yom Kippur fell on the early side that year. The thought of walking into our synagogue, which was affiliated with our Jewish day school and where we knew hundreds of families, with a dress-clad G was starting to freak me out. I knew our temple community would be supportive of our new family; we belonged to a Reform synagogue that prided itself on being socially responsible, socially conscious, and socially active. I'm pretty sure we were one of the first synagogues in the United States to hire a gay female rabbi. And all of the clergy knew about and expressed support of G's impending transition. But we had "ark honors" this Jewish New Year, which meant we'd be called to the front of the sanctuary to open the ark, which held the Torah. It was a big honor—one we'd received before, and one that I 100 percent appreciated, but also one that was, arguably, coming at a less-than-perfect time. The idea of our family being in the spotlight, standing before our congregation on one of the holiest days of the year, just a couple weeks after G officially transitioned made me shiver.

"Oh my God, Mike," I half said, half shouted. "You're not gonna fucking believe this!"

"Kate, language! The kids are in the other room."

"Mike, I don't give a fuck." I was totally losing my cool. "You've got to see this! "Look." I waved my nephew's bar mitzvah invite in front of Mike's face. "It's addressed to the Brookes family," I screamed.

"And?"

"And the invitation sends us to a special website to RSVP," I said, pointing to my computer. "There's like six events we need to reply to . . . the Friday-night dinner, a campfire, the bar mitzvah service . . ."

"Okay," Mike said.

"It's not okay! Look!" I pointed to the screen. "We have to reply to each event individually. The four of us. Me, Katherine; you, Michael; Jacob; and *Jennifer*." I threw my hands up in the air. "Jennifer! They listed G as Jennifer! We haven't even told my stepsister and her husband that G was planning to transition, let alone what her name was gonna be. And they listed her as Jennifer!"

"I guess someone told them," Mike said.

"My parents told them," I screamed. "Obviously! Even after they promised me that they wouldn't! Couldn't they keep their mouths shut just this once?"

I knew so many families at Ackerman who had been shut out from family gatherings and celebrations altogether and would have traded places with me in a heartbeat, but in the avalanche of things I couldn't control about this situation, I had naively thought we at least had timing in our corner.

Mike stood before me looking calm as a cucumber, hiding the anger I assumed he was feeling.

"I'm sorry," I acknowledged. "You were right. They couldn't keep the damn secret."

I went back to my computer and tried to compose a rational email to my stepsister and her husband. Thankfully, it turned out that the RSVP wall wasn't public, so I was not about to be inundated with— what? Congratulations? Commiseration? I wasn't sure I was ready to receive either.

I showed the response to Mike.

"Nice," he said. "She obviously didn't know it wasn't public knowledge yet."

"Agreed," I replied. "But it still overwhelms me. G's in such a precarious place; I just want this to all be—perfect." (Admittedly, a really tall ask for what we were about to go through.) "And besides, her name isn't Jennifer."

That, too, was driving me batty. I'd been relieved when G had finally rejected Jennifer, a name I didn't particularly like, as a possible new name. The problem, however, was that she didn't seem to like *any* of the names she picked for more than a week or two, in some cases less than a day or two.

Mike and I *tried* to keep up with the frequent name changes. But Jacob? Not so much.

"I've known him as Gideon for eight years," Jacob would complain. "How am I supposed to just call him something else? He's Gideon. And he's always gonna be Gideon."

We tried to strike a middle ground with him.

"If you won't call G by the name she wants," I said, "please don't use any name. And definitely don't use Gideon."

"What do you mean?" Jacob asked.

"If you want G to turn on the TV but you don't want to call her 'Bella,' you don't have to say, 'Bella, can you turn on the TV?' Instead, just ask, 'Can *you* please turn on the TV?' without using a specific name. But please don't say, 'Gideon, turn on the TV.'"

"Seriously, Mom?"

"Yes, seriously. I know it's hard, Jacob, but please try."

I empathized with Jacob. I told him it was hard for me to call G by another name too, let alone a female one.

What I didn't tell him was that part of the reason it was so hard for me was because, you know, *I'd picked that name*! We had put *so much* thought into selecting Jacob and Gideon; we'd lain in bed countless nights discussing and writing down different name combinations until we'd arrived at names that we felt fit.

As a "Kate" and "Mike," we'd agreed we preferred Jewish-sounding names and wanted to honor relatives who'd passed away, and we'd also put effort into searching for first/middle combinations that sounded strong together and flowed well with our last name.

I won't pretend our process was any more elaborate than that of other parents-to-be, just that it *was*, indeed, a process. We hadn't wanted to get it wrong. Yet somehow we'd gotten it about as wrong as wrong could get. So I was struggling to let the name Gideon go, but I could also understand the pressure G felt to get her new name just right.

Thankfully, I liked most of the names that followed more than G's initial choice: Elisa, Bella, Phoebe, Liv, Juliette. Mike and I addressed G accordingly but, at her strict instruction, still only in our home and only when our immediate family was present.

On the rare occasion when I *loved* a name, when I felt a real connection, I'd naively tried to push G to feel a similar connection. I definitely applied the full-court press with Arianna.

"OMG, do you remember when we bumped into Arianna Huffington last year?" I asked. "She totally spoke to us!"

"Arianna who?" G asked. "Who the heck is that?"

"Only one of the coolest, most fabulous writers and businesswomen on the planet!" I answered a little too enthusiastically. "Remember when we were in an elevator downtown last fall, after we saw that doctor who told the funny jokes? We were leaving and hopped into the elevator, and a tall, pretty, reddish-blond-haired woman with a gorgeous accent turned to me and said, 'Wow, your son has the most beautiful blue eyes.' Remember, G? And I said to her, 'Thank you, his heart is even more beautiful!'"

"Oh, now I remember! I wrote about it for an assignment in school that day! Her name was Arianna?"

"Yup, and she's an incredible woman! Famous too!"

"Wow." G sounded starstruck.

This is it, I told myself. *Arianna's a lock.*

Three days later, G asked us to call her Charlotte.

Jacob grew angrier with each new name, and G grew more frustrated any time we overruled a new name.

"Why can't I be Anya?" G asked.

"Because your first cousin's name is Anya, remember?"

"Who cares?"

"We care," I said. "We're not picking the name of a close family member."

"Mom, all of the good names are taken!" G screamed.

"Kiddo, there are billions of names out there. I know we can find at least one that you like!"

"Then call me Felicia," she said, stomping away.

I realized I needed to take matters into my own hands. So I scoured baby name websites and began compiling lists. Eight years earlier, when I was pregnant with the twins, this had been one of my favorite activities. This time around, it wasn't nearly as fun.

We weren't alone. Lots of the parents in our trans circle had a tough time with the new name concept. Partly for emotional reasons, but also for practical ones. Some parents, for instance, wanted their kids to pick new names using the same first letter as their old ones, so that even though their gender was changing, their initials would not.

I knew a Sam who'd become Sadie. A Haley who was now Hank.

When Lauren's kid wanted to change his name to Jack, Lauren couldn't have cared less about keeping the original first initial; she was more concerned with how Jack would sync up with their last name. Which was Ashe.

"Nobody will care if my name is Jack Ashe," he argued.

"I care," Lauren said. "Your dad and I didn't birth a Jack Ashe."

That got a laugh.

Shortly thereafter, they arrived at Jared.

My breaking point came right before G was about to start her new school. Back in June, we'd scheduled an August meeting with her new teachers, the school principal, the school psychologist, and G's gender therapist. It would be our chance to check in with the team and let them know how G would identify when she arrived on the first day, and how we would deal with any related issues, like G's pronouns and which bathroom G would use.

Administrators had just one more question for us. What was G's new name?

"Funny you should ask." I sighed. "G has gone through about a dozen but hasn't settled on one yet. We let her know she needs to pick one ASAP!"

"I can imagine it's a big decision," the principal said. "And we're happy to leave her name off of the class lists we send out next week if she hasn't made her final decision. But we will need to know at least two days before school begins, so her teachers can prepare her classroom."

"Totally understandable," I said. "And we appreciate your patience."

"We want G to feel as comfortable here as she can, and we're all here to support her and your family," the principal said. "Why don't you email me by Monday with her new name?"

"Sounds like a plan." I smiled.

Mike and I left the meeting feeling more confident than ever that our daughter was headed to the right school.

We were less confident that she'd settle on a name.

And she *needed* a name—specifically, one that would stick. The only kids we knew whose names changed periodically were other trans kids. And G wasn't planning on going to school as a transgender girl; she was planning to go as a girl. She wanted to go stealth. (Going stealth means for a trans person to live completely as their gender identity and to pass in the public sphere. Outside of their family, most people are unaware that they are trans.)

If G changed her name at school every few weeks, she'd draw attention to herself, making it infinitely more difficult to go stealth. Hence our need for a reasonably permanent name.

‡ ‡

"G told me she's overwhelmed," Olivia told us a few days after our return from Myrtle Beach. "That choosing a new name is a big deal and she's not sure which name to pick. I think she's feeling a lot of pressure."

I was relieved to hear this from our sitter. It meant Mike and I weren't projecting—that the whole name deal wasn't just hard for us, it was also hard for G.

We talked with our gender therapist, and she agreed it was appropriate for me and Mike to step in and guide G's decision. In an effort to make the selection easier, we wrote down five names, all starting with the letter *G*, and presented them to our daughter.

"We want you to make the decision," we assured her. "But we know this is hard for you, so we've given you five awesome names from which to choose. And you can pick any one of them."

"What are the names?" she wisely asked.

"Grace, Gabriella, Gina, Galit, and Gemma," we told her.

"That's all?" she wanted to know.

"Love, that's five names," I coaxed. "You've had months to select one, and we understand how hard it's been. Now's the time. So, yes, these are the five names. Each of them is beautiful. Mommy and Daddy promise you can't go wrong."

"I hate all of them!" G said.

"Well, which one do you hate the least?" Mike wondered aloud.

"Gabriella," she said. But in a tone that seemed to lack commitment or connection to the name.

"Gabriella, wow!" I said with enthusiasm. "I love it, sweetheart. I think that's a beautiful choice for you."

She smiled. Thank God.

‡ ‡

"Gabriella wasn't my top choice," Mike admitted to me privately later that day. "But I know it'll grow on me 'cause I love our daughter."

"Really? It was totally my top choice," I said. "Honestly, I love it! I think it's a gorgeous name."

"And that's what makes horse racing," Mike said with a grin.

We emailed the school to let them know. They thanked us, said they'd add her name to the online class list, and assured us that her name would be on her cubby, her desk, and the door to her classroom when she got to school the first day, just like all of the other kids.

"Just like all of the other kids," the teachers had typed.

Dear God, I thought, *please help my daughter feel "just like all of the other kids."*

19: The Appalachian Trail Takes Manhattan

"Gabriella, are you almost ready to go, love?"

"One minute, Mama!"

I sat at the dining room table, tapping my foot and staring at my watch.

"You'll be on time," Mike said. "Don't worry, Katie."

"Being late is the least of my worries," I told him.

"She's gonna be okay, hon."

"I'm sure she will; it's *me* I'm worried about."

Two minutes later, Gabriella walked into the living room wearing her royal blue–and-white-striped sleeveless hoodie and carrying a small bag.

"Whatcha got in the bag, sweets?" I asked her.

"My girl clothes," she said, smiling just a little.

It was extensions day. I'd barely slept the night before, and I'd woken up that morning feeling exhausted and anxious.

"Are you excited?" I'd asked Gabriella earlier that morning as I popped a Xanax and brought the kids' breakfast to the table.

"I guess." She shrugged. "I just hope they look good."

"You always look good, G. And now, you'll finally have the long hair you've been wanting."

"I can't believe he's getting extensions," Jacob chimed in. "That's the stupidest thing I've ever heard."

"Come on, J-man," I chided him. "We've talked about this. Please be supportive of your sister."

"You mean my brother?" he said with a smirk.

"You know what I mean, Jacob. Be nice."

‡ ‡

Gabriella held my hand as we walked out of our building, turned onto Broadway, and headed toward the hair salon. It was the end of August. Warmish and sunny, but I could feel fall approaching.

"Get comfortable," Traffic said as G sat in the chair. "This could take a while."

"How long are we thinking?" I asked. "About three hours or so?"

"Maybe a little less," Traffic answered. "We'll see how it goes."

As Gabriella got settled into her salon chair, I thought back to a couple I'd met recently at Ackerman. Their daughter had spent about two years growing out her hair, yet the couple still hadn't told their parents their child was trans. The grandparents lived in Europe, and when the family Skyped, their daughter wore a baseball hat to cover her hair and pretended she was still a boy.

I glanced at Gabriella and was grateful that she'd no longer have to pretend to be someone she wasn't. If she was nervous, the kid didn't show it. She sat like a champ. Super still. Shoulders back. Not one complaint about how long the process was taking or the physical pressure Traffic had to use in order to apply the extensions to G's existing hair.

There truly wasn't much for me to do but sit and wait. I checked Facebook. I played games on my phone. I group chatted with a few friends who knew about Gabriella's plan.

Me: It's finally happening. We're at the extension place.

K: Wow, exciting!!

Me: It's something all right . . .

S: How's G?

Me: G's actually doing great. Not sure I've ever seen a kid with ADHD sit still for so long.

K: LOL!!! How are you?

Me: Pretty much a basket case. G's been a girl at home . . . but she's coming out to the rest of the world when we walk out of here today. Even brought a change of clothes.

J: That's huge.

Me: Yup.

K: Keep us posted! G's gonna do great!! She's so lucky to have you and Mike for her parents.

Me: Eh, the parent part is debatable. But I know G will rock it!!!

‡ ‡

Three hours and lots of hair later, G looked like she *literally* might rock it. The extensions were long. Really long. And they were certainly pretty enough. Real hair. Hair that matched G's own color almost exactly. Except . . .

Imagine a kid with almost-shoulder-length hair.

Imagine adding super long hair to the same kid.

Now imagine how the shorter hair blends in with the longer hair.

Exactly. It doesn't.

Three hours and hundreds of dollars later, and my new daughter was rockin' a mullet.

I held my breath.

But you know what? Gabriella loved it. She spent several minutes striking poses and admiring her long locks in the mirror before leaving Traffic's station. Traffic took pictures. I took pictures. Gabriella took pictures.

Then she grabbed her bag, hopped into the bathroom, took off the hoodie, and walked out of the restroom wearing a pink-and-white tie-dyed T-shirt from Justice and matching leggings.

This was it. My first walk in public with my daughter.

The journey home felt strangely longer than the hair appointment itself.

Were people staring at my new daughter? Did they know something was different?

Did Gabriella feel different?

I know I did. Almost like butterflies, but not just in my stomach: they creeped all the way up my chest and into my throat, giving me a quasi-nauseated, light-headed sensation that would linger for about the next month or two.

‡ ‡

"Wow, look at you," Dr. Cara said when she opened the door to the waiting room later that day. "Your hair looks beautiful!"

"Thank you," Gabriella said. "I really love it."

"And you came here wearing your girl clothes," she pointed out.

"Yup."

"How do you feel?" Dr. Cara asked.

"Good, I guess," Gabriella answered. "I really like my hair." And then, "Can you take some more pictures, Mommy?"

"Of course I will!" First, I snapped a couple shots with her hair down. The kid genuinely looked happy.

Then I had an idea.

"Why don't you try putting on the pink headband that matches your shirt?" I suggested. We'd brought a bunch of hair accessories with us to our appointment. G pulled out a headband and a brush from her backpack and began brushing her hair.

"Be careful!" I reminded her. "We need to be gentle with the extensions."

"I know, Mom," she said, half rolling her eyes. Then she slid the headband over her hair and pushed it back about an inch beyond her front hairline, just behind her ears.

She smiled. I smiled. Dr. Cara smiled.

And then I almost cried.

"My god, sweetheart," I said. "Look at you; you are simply stunning."

And she was. I felt like I was seeing my daughter for the first time. Her bright blue eyes; her wide, toothy smile; her newly long hair falling naturally from the headband, over her shoulders, and halfway down her back.

My daughter was beautiful.

And she was happy.

And the hair extensions were just what she'd needed to face the world as a girl.

‡ ‡

Gabriella hasn't worn her striped hoodie since that day. But she still keeps it tucked in a dresser drawer and won't let us throw it away.

One time I asked her why.

"It's special to me, Mom," she told me. "I wore it the day I became a girl."

Part Three
Our Son and Daughter

20: Dear Friends, Family, Doormen, and All 743 Residents of Our Co-Op

When it comes to my life, I'm pretty open. I don't hide much, don't get embarrassed by much, and, on the contrary, sometimes inadvertently make others uncomfortable by saying too much.

Want to know what meds I take? I'll tell you.

How many men I've slept with? I can estimate.

But *my* business and my *kids'* business are two separate beasts.

Still, with the extensions firmly in place ("Gabriella, please stop tugging your hair!"), Mike and I figured it was time to tell our circle.

We'd been crafting an email for months. Had even sent a preliminary one to the clergy at our synagogue over the summer to give them a confidential heads-up. But this note was different. Mike and I planned to send it to the parents of the kids' entire grade at their Jewish day school before classes began that fall.

We wouldn't be sending *any* note to the parents at Gabriella's new school, where she was planning to go stealth and where only a handful of kids had known "Gideon" previously. Yet here we were, sending an email to dozens of parents at her old school—announcing her transition.

But how could we not? Gabriella had known many of these families since she was two. She'd made her best friends at this school. Mike and I had become close friends with many of the parents. And perhaps most importantly, Jacob was still attending the school, and we needed to make sure his transition to third grade went as smoothly as possible. Could you imagine the confusion if Gabriella, sporting her long hair and purple sundress, came to pick up Jacob after school and no one knew Jacob's brother was now his sister? Exactly. We couldn't do that to Jacob. Or to Gabriella.

Hence the email. Which would also give parents the chance to discuss the change with their kids in their own homes and on their own terms.

I was simultaneously excited and petrified the moment I pressed send.

From: Kate Brookes
Sent: Monday, September 4, 2017 4:51
Subject: New beginnings in the Brookes family

Hey, friends! Hope everyone had a great summer. :)

Mike and I wanted to reach out before classes begin and let you know what's going on in our world. Jacob is super excited to be returning for third grade. He'll be in class with some of your kids . . . and looks forward to playdates with many more of them.

We've also got a couple of big changes we want to share. First, Gideon, as most of you know, will be starting at a new school in September and, while a little nervous, is mostly excited.

Second, we want you to know that Gideon socially transitioned to a girl over the summer and her name is now Gabriella (Gabby or G for short). Essentially, what this means is that Gabriella now identifies as a girl—she's continuing to grow her hair; she's "shopped till she's dropped" and now dresses in typical girl clothing; she is calling herself by a female name, Gabriella (**it's possible this name could change—she's been "trying out" names for months); and she is using female pronouns to describe herself. And she has asked that everyone do the same (address her as Gabriella, Gabby, or G and use female pronouns with her).

This change probably won't come as a huge surprise to many of you; Gabriella has been gender-nonconforming for years, and we are proud that she has embraced who she is and we fully support her in every way!

Although Gabriella will no longer be at school with your kids, she hopes to maintain her many friendships. Mike and I realize that for some of your kids, her new identity may prove too uncomfortable for their young friendships to handle. While we will be sad if/when this happens, we get it, and we will not judge where your kids fall on this spectrum. We only ask that you encourage your kids to be respectful to Gabriella and to Jacob.

Our family has found a support system to help us through this transition, and we've learned (and continue to learn) about transgender children and language to use when discussing them with other kids. Chances are, you may not have as much information about this as we do. If you need some help, or have questions, we are happy to speak to you and/or point you to good resources.

Gabriella's transition has been pretty tough for eight-year-old Jacob, who is mourning the loss of his twin brother. (Candidly, it hasn't been a cakewalk for us either, and we're significantly older than eight.) We're confident that with time, Jacob will realize he's gained not only a sister but a happier twin. For right now, though, he is clearly struggling with the change.

If your kids ask about Jacob, you can let them know he's the same boy he's always been . . . and always will be. He's still awesome, loves sports, is super smart and super funny. And he's even taller than he was before school let out for the summer.

If your kids ask about Gabriella, you can tell them that she is now living life as the person she believes she was meant to be—a girl. Gender identity aside, she is much the same as she's always been: she's still awesome, still creative, beautiful, silly, artistic, and a lover of all things princess, pink, and lilac—just like before.

When you and your kids see either Gabriella or Jacob, we'd kindly ask you to not make a big production and to try to keep things as "normal" as possible. There's some self-consciousness all around, and we're sure if J and/or G want to talk about it, they will bring it up.

So that's where we are—for now. It's been quite a journey. And we realize this is just the beginning.

We look forward to seeing you soon.

Sincerely,

Kate and Mike (Jacob and Gabriella's proud parents!)

It took only a few minutes for the responses to start flooding our inbox.

"Thank you so much for sharing these beginnings with us. Gabriella is very brave, and I see how proud you are of her."

"Hats off for this courageous step and email explanation. We can only imagine how complex and challenging this must have been. The world around her will adapt and take to a happy girl more readily than to an uncomfortable boy. So, here's to new beginnings!"

"Absolutely BEAUTIFULLY written and I'm crying as I type this. Mason can't wait to hang out with Jacob soon and he's super psyched to have Gabriella in religious school. Which is probably the only thing Mason likes about religious school."

"WOW! What a beautiful, clear, articulate note. THANK YOU for sharing this. I can't imagine what it was like to write this, much less to experience it. I feel very lucky to have your family in my family's life!"

The responses were both overwhelming and overwhelmingly positive. Not that we were surprised. These were our people—mine, Mike's, Jacob's, and Gabriella's. If *they* didn't react favorably, who would? Still, we appreciated each and every thoughtful note. I sometimes look back at these emails to affirm how far we've all come.

‡ ‡

Telling our friends and family was one thing; determining which other people in our circle to tell—and how to do it—was a bit trickier. We lived in an NYC high-rise building—354 units with a facade that spanned an entire block. The building staff alone topped twenty, and that didn't include the garage attendants. We didn't feel compelled to send all of these people a personal note; half of them probably had no clue who we were. But we did want to avoid awkward moments in the lobby.

I remember the day I told my favorite doorman.

"Good morning!" Claude said as I stepped off the elevator, a warm, genuine smile taking over his face. "How are you and your beautiful kids today!"

"We're all good, thanks, Claude. How are you?"

"Doing well, thanks for asking! Can I get you a cab today?"

"No," I said with a little twinge of trepidation, "but I would like to talk with you if you have a couple minutes."

He nodded, and I launched in. When I was done, he nodded again. "Thank you for telling me," he said. "How is Jacob doing?"

"That's awesome of you to ask, Claude," I said, touched. "Thank you. He's having a pretty rough time with all of this, but he'll be okay."

"With you and Mike as parents, I'm sure they'll both be okay," he said.

I gave him a hug, did my best to hold back my tears, and ran out to grab a cup of coffee.

Once again, we were pretty lucky.

‡ ‡

And our luck held. Even through some slightly awkward encounters. A girl from camp who ran up to us on the street and was momentarily confused by "Gideon's" appearance. A neighbor who asked me where the boys were as I was walking out the door with Gabriella. And a kindergartner in the playroom who repeatedly shouted, "You're not Gabriella, you're Gideon!" in Gabriella's face.

Then there was the time I got in the elevator to go to the gym.

Jillian, another acquaintance from the building, was already in the car and started chatting me up. "How are you?" she asked.

"Good," I said. "How are you? How is your son? I haven't seen him for a while."

"Oh, Noah." She sighed. "He's in Utah for a few months. He's okay now, thank God. But it hasn't been an easy road. How are your boys?"

I knew Jillian had gotten divorced a few years before, and I guessed it had been hard on Noah. Whenever I'd seen them in the elevator together since the divorce, they'd always been arguing, and Noah had seemed down. I had no idea what he was doing in Utah, but I sensed it wasn't a planned vacation.

"I hear you about it not being an easy road," I said, trying to empathize. "I'm sure your kiddo will be okay. And I get it. One of my sons is now my daughter."

"Really," she said, sounding strangely concerned.

"Really." I nodded. "But she seems happy, so that's a good thing. Have a great day."

The car stopped at the gym and I walked out. I was already opening the door to the little cardio room when I heard Jillian call my name. I turned around to find she'd followed me off the elevator.

"I'm only saying this because I like you, Kate," she said in a low voice. "But I really think that what your son is doing is dangerous."

"Dangerous?" I replied.

"Yes, and before you make any decisions that I'm sure you'll regret, I'd like to share a book with you. Do you mind if I leave it for you at the front desk?"

"Umm, sure," I told her, wondering (a) what sort of book she wanted to share, (b) why she was convinced my daughter's transition was dangerous, and (c) how she thought reading some book would change our situation.

"I'm always a fan of information," I told her. "It can't hurt to see another perspective, right?"

"Again, Kate, it's because I like you, and I think you'll really want to read it," Jillian assured me.

"Okay, then, great. Thanks. I'll look out for it." I waved goodbye and slipped in my earbuds.

‡ ‡

Three days later, one of our doormen stopped me at the front desk.

"Hey, Kate, Jillian left this book for you."

"Thanks," I said, taking the book. I glanced at the front cover as I headed for the elevator. *When Harry Became Sally*, by Ryan T. Anderson. I took out my phone and googled Anderson and the book.

"Ahh, I get it now," I said out loud.

Anderson was one of the most prominent voices in the anti-LGBTQ movement, and his book was an attempt to convince people to reject the legitimacy of transgender identities. I sat on the bench outside the elevator landing when I reached my floor, simultaneously flipping through the pages and googling more.

Not for nothing, but this Anderson guy was really blunt. In the intro, he writes: "In this book, I argue that Dr. McHugh got it right"— referring to Dr. Paul McHugh, who theorized that being transgender is a mental illness.

I showed the book to Mike when I got back to our apartment. He was outraged.

"You know she's ultra-religious and her husband left her for another man, right?"

My eyes widened. "No, I didn't know that. I only know that she's got a son who's always been nice to me in the elevator but who she seems to yell at a lot. But whatever. I'd rather people are honest with us, Mike, instead of saying shit behind our backs."

"You're a much nicer person than I am," he said. "I would have told her to go to hell."

"It's a big world out there, Mike. We can't tell it all to go to hell."

‡ ‡

Of course, hell was where many of the loudest folks in the anti-trans community said Gabriella was going—along with Mike and me, for enabling her transition. Focus on the Family and the Family Research Council, two of the largest and most well-funded Christian right groups, had recently worked together first to find obscure and out-dated theories to pathologize transgender people and then to outline a strategy for pushing anti-trans policy and legislation.[1]

These groups then applauded the Trump administration when, in the two-month period preceding my daughter's transition, it added three more anti-transgender actions to its already growing list of attacks on the LGBTQ community. On July 26, 2017, Trump tweeted that "the United States Government will not accept or allow Transgender individuals to serve in any capacity in the US Military." On August 25, he released a memo directing the Defense Department to create a plan to discharge all transgender military members and maintain a recruitment ban.[2] Then on September 7, three days after I sent our letter to Jacob's school, the Justice Department filed a brief in the Supreme Court arguing for a constitutional right allowing businesses to discriminate on the basis of sexual orientation and, implicitly, gender identity.

So, yes, I was relieved our friends reacted positively to our letter announcing Gabriella's transition. And yes, I knew a few awkward encounters, including one with an extraordinarily nosey neighbor, were really just that: awkward. But I also realized that right now my family was living in a bubble, and there were literally hundreds of thousands, if not millions, of people who would rather strip my daughter of her rights and dignity than see her as the girl I knew her to be. Which meant my job of protecting my child—making sure she had that happy, healthy, *normal* childhood I'd promised myself I'd give her—had just gotten a lot more challenging.

21: Snap and Post

A pple picking, the first day of school, Halloween.

According to the unwritten, though largely understood, laws of modern-day parenting, new parents are required not only to participate in these rituals with their children but also to document them and post pictures concurrently. I didn't even know apple picking was a thing until my sister-in-law posted the cutest shots on Facebook of my niece and nephew riding a tractor and eating apples at some obscure farm in northwest New Jersey about eight years ago. And of course, once we had our twins, we jumped at the chance to join the bandwagon.

First day of school?

Snap and post.

Obviously.

I had a good friend from college who got married relatively late in life and gave birth to her son even later. This year, she posted the cutest picture of her little towhead holding a handmade sign that read, "First day of preschool, August 28, 2017." The caption underneath: "I've been waiting years to be able to post this picture like all of my other friends."

I remember feeling the same way when I designed, ordered, and sent our family's first New Year's card after giving birth to the twins. "Look, we're finally parents!" the card seemed to scream. "Now *we* can send out holiday cards like the rest of the families we know!"

So, two weeks after we arrived home from Myrtle Beach, I set my alarm a little early to make sure I had time to shower, blow out my hair, and feed Jacob breakfast before we headed off to his first day of third grade and took the obligatory pictures to mark the occasion.

It was the first time I'd be taking a first-day-of-school picture that didn't include Gideon. And not just because Gideon was now Gabriella; her new school didn't start until the following day. It felt strange heading down to our building's lobby with just one kid. As did taking a picture of just one kid.

All of which was nothing compared to the strangeness of approaching the school. It was like a slow-motion Brain DePalma nightmare. I felt all of the parents either staring at me and Jacob or trying *not* to stare at me and Jacob.

Would the kids ask Jacob about his sister? Would they make fun of him? Did all of their parents tell their kids about Gabriella?

I walked Jacob to his classroom, something parents are only invited to do on the first day, introduced myself to his teachers, and hugged and kissed many of the moms and dads I hadn't seen all summer.

I tried to smile, to play things cool, to pretend that my heart wasn't beating so hard that I had broken into fear sweat.

"How *are* you?"

"So good to see you."

"Are you okay? How's Jacob?"

Their heads tilted as they asked these questions like this was the first day of shiva.

A few minutes after entering Jacob's class, as my forced smile started to physically hurt, I hugged Jacob goodbye and wished him a great day. I headed out of the school praying, *Please, dear God, let Jacob have an okay day today, and please, please, please let the kids be nice to him.*

Subject: Re: Welcome to Room 313!

Hi, Kate and Mike,

Thank you so much for your detailed emails and reflections on Jacob. We really loved meeting him (and you) today.

We did overhear one or two kids expressing their curiosity today and asking Jacob questions about Gabriella. As far as we could tell, the kids seemed to be genuinely interested and were not teasing Jacob in any way. Jacob handled it well, and we spoke quickly with the students about respecting people's privacy; to that end, we suggested that we only talk about another person's family life if that person brings it up. We will continue to follow the guidelines you put forth in the email and keep an eye on things to make sure that students are allowing Jacob his privacy when he wants it.

We look forward to a wonderful year and can't wait for day 2 tomorrow!

Best,

Rebecca & Molly

Thank. Fucking. God.

Still, I sipped my second glass of cabernet and proceeded to lie awake most of the night.

‡ ‡

In the morning Gabriella was "nerva-cited." Super nervous, but really excited. She'd laid out her outfit the night before and was already getting dressed when I popped into her room. "How are you, beautiful? Ready for your big day?"

"I guess," she said. "But I really wish I was going back to my old school."

"I know, it can feel weird to go to a new school. But my prediction is you'll love it!"

It was chilly for early September—not too cold for her favorite white cutoffs with the embroidered edges, bright pink shirt, and light pink leather high-tops with pink pom-poms, but cold enough that she threw on her new turquoise hoodie before slinging her new, rainbow-themed backpack over her shoulders.

Mike and I walked her to the lobby and out the front door, and then I announced it was time for first-day-of-school pictures.

"Smile, gorgeous!" I instructed enthusiastically. "Just a couple; I promise!"

I must have snapped a half dozen or so in less than a minute.

Then I toggled from the camera app to the picture app and gave a look. I hated all of them.

"Just one more," I said, as Gabriella flipped her hair and gave a little smile.

"Phew," I thought. *This one should work.*

And then I stood back a little to catch a glimpse—and take one more shot—of Gabriella and Mike as they started the trek to school, side by side, before jogging up to join them and grabbing Gabriella's hand.

Her new school was only four blocks and one avenue from our apartment. Kids trekked from all over the city to go to this school for bright students with learning disabilities. And here it was, in our own backyard.

Still, as we walked toward the entrance, I couldn't help but feel that the school, the day itself, even my daughter, were a world away. Far from what I had imagined when I found out we were finally pregnant, when I read all of those "what to expect" books, when I listened to all my friends' stories about giving birth and raising their kids. Not one of them had told me that one day I might be walking my child—my child with a new name, a new gender, and new hair—to a new school. Not one of the books had suggested this was even a possibility, let alone given me any advice or suggestions on what to do or how I should feel about it if this day came.

When we finally arrived, I wrapped Gabriella in a big hug and told her that I loved her and we were super proud of her. Mike did the same, and then we watched as she half walked, half skipped into the building. Her new school didn't allow parents to take their kids to classrooms—even on the first day, and even if their kids had a new first name and a new gender.

Mike took my hand as we turned to go. "You okay?"

"I'm not," I told him and started to cry.

We started walking.

"What am I supposed to do about first-day-of-school pictures?" I asked him through tears.

"What do you mean?" he asked, genuinely confused.

"I always post pictures of the kids on the first day of school. I posted one of Jacob yesterday. Do I post a picture of Gabriella?" I asked. "Would that be outing her?"

No comment.

"What am I supposed to do, Mike?" I asked again.

Mike was thinking.

"Well, you posted pics of Super J, right?" he finally asked.

"Right."

I could almost see the gears grinding in Mike's mind as he sifted through a mental spreadsheet. *There's a picture tab for Jacob*, I imagined him thinking. *So . . .*

"Then I think you post one of Gabriella," he said.

And then, twenty or so seconds later, he added, "We posted our son, so we post our daughter."

So, I stopped walking about a block away from our apartment and looked at the pictures I'd just taken. I used the one with Mike, cropped him out, centered Gabriella, and prepped the picture to post.

Now I needed a caption.

What was I supposed to say?

"First day of school for my daughter"?

"Hello, world, one of my sons is now my daughter"?

"My new daughter and her new mullet head to school"?

That last one made me laugh out loud.

And then I started typing. "And she's off! First day of 3rd grade for Gabriella ☺ #ProudMom."

Click.

I had just posted the first pictures of my daughter on Facebook.

22: I'm Only Telling My Best Friends

Both kids seemed to be adjusting to our new arrangement. Mike, meanwhile, was staying busy at work, and I was staying busy distracting myself with anything but work while at work.

"Katie, I think someone hacked our credit card again," Mike said one night in early October.

"Yikes. How much?" I asked.

"One hundred nineteen dollars and ninety-nine cents."

"On what?"

"Sega charges? Maybe iTunes?"

"Huh? Let me see that," I said, looking at the bank statement on his computer screen. "Yeah." I sighed. "We weren't hacked."

Mike looked at me funny.

"That was me. I've been buying lives."

"Buying lives?"

"In Farmville. It's like a spin-off of Candy Crush."

"You spent a hundred and twenty dollars on Farmville?"

"Nope. I spent one hundred nineteen dollars and ninety-nine cents," I replied with a smile. "I'm sorry. I'll stop buying so many lives. It's just . . . I'm having a hard time concentrating at work." *Or anywhere.* "And when that happens, I sit around and overthink everything, which makes me sad. So, instead, I play Farmville."

"Oh."

"And Farmville is fun; it keeps me from thinking too much."

"Got it. I just want to make sure—"

"Don't worry, Mike, I'll cut back on the lives. Promise."

"Thanks," he said in a tone I didn't find particularly thankful.

"Gabriella has a playdate later this week," I said, trying to change the subject. "With a girl at her new school. She invited her for the afternoon and dinner."

"That's awesome! Anyone special?"

"Lizzie, the one whose mom reached out to me the other day."

"The one Gabriella *told*?"

"That's the one." I smiled.

"Well, I guess your email went over pretty well, then."

"I guess it did."

I was fast becoming a pro at crafting emails to concerned and/or curious parents. Specifically, those whose children came home from school reporting that their new friend in school was a "girl with a penis" or a "girl who used to be a boy." Of course, the school would neither confirm nor deny the gender identity of our daughter when asked, but the school did reach out to us (on numerous occasions) when a parent inquired and asked how/if we'd like to address said inquiry. I always responded the same way—by thanking the principal/ teacher/administrator who called and letting them know I'd be happy to talk to any parent who had questions.

It was a minor miracle I didn't field more questions, given the school's parent portal. Lizzie's mom had tipped me off before our daughters' second playdate. She'd logged on to the portal to confirm our address, and when she clicked on my name, it had listed our child as "Gideon." I'd thanked her for the heads-up and immediately called the school.

During the 2017–2018 school year, the Department of Education still recognized our daughter as our son. By New York City law, schools couldn't change a student's birth name to their preferred name without a court order and/or a new birth certificate. We still didn't have either.

Even so, when we noticed the discrepancy on the school intranet, our school changed G's name to Gabriella within fifteen minutes. The principal even apologized to us for the error.

"Not your fault," I assured her. We'd needed to approve all of our family information, and it appeared Mike and I had missed that entry. "Thanks so much for making the change so quickly!"

New York City schools, I'd learned, were among the best in the nation—on paper, at least—when it came to supporting transgender kids. The NYC DOE had released new protocols the previous spring requiring teachers to identify transgender students using their preferred pronouns.[1]

Among the guidelines, teachers and staff were instructed to

- be supportive of trans students, "including those going through a gender transition"

- defend them from bullies

- "honor a student's request to be referred to by the name and gender that corresponds to their gender identity"

- use students' preferred names and genders on student IDs and in the majority of school records

- permit trans students to "participate in physical education and intramural sports in accordance with the student's gender identity"

- allow them access to facilities—including restrooms, locker rooms, and changing rooms—that corresponded with their gender identity

- allow them to participate in all school activities, including "overnight field trips"

- accept trans students into all-girls or all-boys schools based on which gender they'd chosen

Beyond that, DOE officials said principals at each school were "responsible for ensuring that all staff are made aware of these guidelines and for making staff aware of appropriate training."

Around this time, local ACLU head Donna Lieberman issued a statement saying, "These new guidelines are a leap forward for transgender students' right to be themselves in New York City schools." She continued, "This is all the more important in the wake of the Trump regime's cruel moves last week to rescind similar guidelines at the federal level."[2] Lieberman added, however, that the city should make it easier for gender-nonconforming students to update past school records to reflect their current identity.

Yet again, we were fortunate that Gabriella's new school had already painted itself an ally (the Center for Inclusion and Social Change defines an ally as "a person who is not LGBTQ but shows support for LGBTQ people and promotes equality in a variety of ways"[3]), regardless of city, state, or federal guidelines.

Mike and I recognized that calling Gabriella by her preferred name and pronouns, encouraging her to use the restroom of her choice (not just one of several gender-inclusive restrooms in the building), and correcting *our mistake* on the parent portal were just a few of the ways in which her school was an ally.

DOE guidelines notwithstanding, not every transgender student in NYC was nearly as fortunate. We'd met a mom in one of our support groups with a transgender daughter not only whose pronouns were not respected but whose safety was clearly in jeopardy at her school. The mom spoke of repeated verbal abuse from fellow students and, perhaps more troubling, from teachers. The support group facilitator had asked the mom to stay after our session one night so they could talk with her one-on-one about intervening on her behalf, setting up some training sessions for school staff, and informing her about her and her daughter's rights.

I remember thinking, *This is New York, one of the most progressive cities in the world, and this woman's poor kid is being bullied?* I could only imagine what it must be like for kids in more conservative cities and/or kids living with parents who didn't support their transition. Except I didn't have to imagine. I only needed to pick up a newspaper or log on to one of my private support groups to see/read about the discrimination and, at times, the abuse.

‡ ‡

I wasn't surprised that Gabriella wanted to tell more than a handful of her new friends about her "secret." I understood her desire for transparency. She wanted her new friends to know her, really know her. But I was concerned.

The problem was that she wanted to be in complete control of who knew what. In her eight-year-old framework, her school friends seemed like a very controlled group. But New York City is very small in certain circles. Some of these kids would splinter off to different middle schools or high schools and attend camps and afterschool programs with kids we didn't know—kids whose paths she would cross after puberty, when that sweet transparency might evaporate. And there would be no un-ringing this bell.

"Hon, have you told lots of kids at your new school that you used to be Gideon?" I asked her one night after dinner.

"Not a lot," she replied. "I'm only telling my closest friends."

And then she rattled off a list of girls she'd told. I knew most of them, and I'd already spoken to most of their moms. But a few caught me off guard.

"They're all your 'closest' friends?"

"Yup, why?"

"It's just that the more people you tell, love, the more people will know."

"Well, they all promised not to tell *anyone*," she said defensively.

"I'm not saying you did anything wrong, G. I just don't want you to be upset if more people find out."

"They won't, Mom!" she screamed. "They promised they wouldn't tell!"

"I know, Gabriella. And I bet they'll try really hard to keep it a secret. But it can be hard for eight-year-olds to keep secrets sometimes. And I don't want you to be sad if people who you haven't told find out."

The anger left her. "Okay, Mama."

‡ ‡

I'll never really be sure who knows what, but I can guarantee more people know Gabriella is trans than she thinks know. I knew I couldn't expect the kids she entrusted with her secret not to slip on occasion, because *I* slipped on occasion. Just a week earlier, she and I had been at a playground with another one of her new school friends and her mom.

"Mommy, why can't you put my hair in a French braid like Zoe's?" G had asked.

"Yikes, kiddo, you know your mom sucks at hair stuff," I'd said with a laugh. "Want to watch a YouTube tutorial with me later?"

It would be like the old days, I thought. When G would watch hairstyling videos and dream of having long locks.

"I could put your hair in a French braid, Gabriella," Zoe's mom offered.

"Could you?" G asked eagerly.

"Of course! Come on over." She motioned for G to come sit in front of her.

"You know what, G," I said quickly, "why don't you and Zoe hit the swings for a few minutes, and then Jill can French braid your hair?"

"But she just said she'd do it," G whined.

"And she will," I insisted. "After you two go on the swings."

"Fine," G grumbled. "Let's go, Zoe."

"So, not sure if you knew this already, but Gabriella has extensions," I whispered to Jill after the girls ran off. "I didn't want you to freak out when you felt her hair. Not that you would, but . . ."

"Ahh, no problem," Jill said, looking at Gabriella and Zoe on the swings. "I can still put her hair in a French braid, even with the extensions." And then her expression shifted, like she was trying to fit the pieces of a puzzle together.

"Gabriella is transgender," I blurted out. "She was Gideon until she started school this year. We got the extensions because she thought she needed longer hair to be a girl, and she got tired of waiting for it to grow."

Momentary silence.

"Wow, the extensions are really beautiful," Jill said.

I wondered if the "wow" was really about the extensions.

"Well, the extensions turned out a bit more mullet-like than we were aiming for." I chuckled. "But Gabriella seems happy enough, so I guess that's a start."

Jill just looked at the girls and smiled. "She does seem pretty happy."

"Do you think Zoe knows?" I asked Jill. "That Gabriella is trans."

"I don't think so," Jill replied. "And I certainly didn't know. Though to be honest, I'm not sure Zoe even knows what transgender is."

"Yeah, Gabriella didn't know what it was either," I admitted. "Until she realized she *was* trans."

We talked a little more about G's transition before the girls ran over.

"Come here, girlfriend," Jill said to G. "Why don't I braid your hair now?"

"Definitely." Gabriella grinned. "Thank you so much!"

Gabriella left the playdate happy; I left wondering if I should have told Jill about Gabriella. She and Zoe were not super close friends; neither were me and Zoe's mother. But I felt I needed to say something to protect my daughter (or at least her hair).

Or maybe I just didn't want to "get caught." Similar to the way Gabriella liked to control who knew what about her, I was realizing that I did too. I wanted to control the narrative. *Her* narrative, admittedly, but mine too. And it threw me off when I didn't have the opportunity to craft the story.

‡ ‡

At a birthday party that fall, a handful of parents I'd never met before were in attendance.

"Have you considered joining the diversity committee?" some woman who I'd never laid eyes on before asked me.

"No, I hadn't really thought about it," I told her, my smile frozen.

"It's just, you might be able to offer a different perspective than most of the other parents." And then she inched closer to me and whispered, "You know, different than parents of cisgender kids." She read my face and put her hand on my arm. "I'm a therapist. I could tell from the first day of school that Gabriella was trans. You know—the hair, the long legs."

I wanted to say, "It's funny—as a therapist, I'd think you'd have more tact than to tell a mom you've never met that her transgender daughter stuck out like a sore thumb. Do patients really pay you?" But I could tell I was being overly sensitive and instead just quickly excused myself.

Then I looked around the room, wondering who knew about Gabriella and who didn't. Was it "news" that a trans kid recently joined the school? Did parents talk about my daughter? Did they talk about me?

Sometimes my child's third grade felt like my third grade all over again.

23: Gabriella, Please Don't Argue with the TSA

M ike and I have only a few guiding rules in our relationship. If you get hit by a car while crossing the street, even if you're not hurt or didn't have the right of way, remember to get the contact information of the offending driver.

Make sure you have the current address and phone number of your dear friend before you drive the hour and a half to meet her and her husband for dinner.

Never intentionally start an argument and/or pick a fight with someone who has the authority to make you or your family's life miserable.

To be fair, the first two rules are relatively straightforward; I probably should have been less worried about the emotional state of the octogenarian who clipped me while I was sipping coffee and crossing Amsterdam and more concerned about my potentially broken foot. And I will always remember that Karen and Daren lived at 4 Marcus Square after circling her neighborhood for forty-five minutes that cold, windy night in December ("I'm pretty sure there's a CVS right near her house, Mike." "Pretty sure, Katie? Seriously!?").

But I'll admit I do still have the occasional issue with authority. Not all authority. And not all the time. Just when I think the authority in question is acting like a moron. Like that time when, three days before we got married, I might've been a tad sarcastic with the woman at the marriage license department. To this day, Mike refers to it as "the day Katie almost kept us from getting legally married."

The point is that I still need to bite my lip occasionally when dealing with certain people in charge. And our kids? Well, they might have inherited my anti-authority tendencies, which can and does make post-9/11 airport travel somewhat challenging.

"Kids, keep your hands to yourselves and stay in line," I reminded them as we entered the security queue at LaGuardia Airport in November.

"We're not stupid, Mom," Jacob grumbled.

"You know we've flown before," Gabriella added, rolling her eyes. "Like a thousand times."

We were finally headed to our cousin Benny's bar mitzvah in Texas, our first foray into flying with Gabriella. And let's just say I was *stressed*. About all of it. Seeing certain family members, spending a weekend at a "sleepaway camp" during the off-season, and—most imminently—making it through the security line.

"You have all of our tickets, love?"

"I do," Mike said.

"Our car rental info?"

"Yup."

"Copies of the kids' birth certificates?"

"Katie, I've got everything."

"Everything with Gabriella's *old name* on it," I whispered to him.

"It'll be fine, I promise," Mike whispered back.

"I hope you're right."

We called her Gabriella. Her *teachers* called her Gabriella. Her *friends* called her Gabriella. But according to her birth certificate and the TSA, she was still Gideon. And that, I feared, could pose a problem. I was also dreading what could happen when my daughter walked through the body scanner.

The hashtag #TravelingWhileTrans had begun trending a

couple of years earlier, in 2015, after a transgender woman named Shadi Petosky was stopped at the Orlando Airport by TSA agents who flagged her crotch as an "anomaly." Shadi claimed she was then harassed by a police officer, held for forty minutes in a screening room, and subjected to a full-body pat down. Further, a bomb expert went through each piece of her luggage, searching for explosives. She not only missed her flight; she was also publicly outed. And not because she posed any threat to her fellow airline passengers; simply because she was a woman with a penis, and TSA workers (a) weren't trained on how to respond to the "anomaly" on their computer screen and (b) when they did respond, they did so haphazardly, insensitively, and, LGBTQ activists argued, unlawfully.[1]

I didn't care that Petosky's ill treatment was not necessarily the norm for trans travelers. I now had a child who was not the norm, and the airport represented one more place where I wasn't sure I could keep my daughter safe. I was quickly learning that so many of the day-to-day experiences I'd always had the privilege to take for granted were now going to be more complicated for my child. That even the most banal activities—like going through a TSA checkpoint—could pose a threat to the trans community.

As we inched closer to the row of TSA employees checking tickets and IDs, I looked at my daughter and wondered what other road-blocks she'd encounter on her new journey. And how many—if any—I could save her from. I felt my armpits start to drip.

"Mom, can you carry my backpack? It's really heavy."

"Jacob, I've got my own backpack and computer to carry. Why don't you try dragging your bag on the floor instead?" I suggested, a sure sign that I was stressed.

"Forget it. I'll just carry the stupid backpack." Jacob scowled.

"Want me to carry it?" Gabriella asked.

"That's super sweet of you to offer, G, but we all need to carry our own stuff in the airport. That's our family rule." And then I inched closer to her and whispered, "And remember, G, when the TSA asks your name, you have to say, 'Gideon.'"

"I'm not saying that, Mom. That's not my name."

"I get it, G, I really do, but—"

"You don't get it, Mom," she said, loudly enough that the family standing behind us in line had to pretend they weren't listening.

"Gabriella, please just don't argue with the TSA," I implored her. "Let's just make it through security, fly to Texas, and have a fun weekend."

Three minutes later, the TSA attendant waved us over. Jacob dragged his backpack, Gabriella huffed and puffed her way to the checkpoint, I wiped my brow, and Mike handed over our tickets to the taker like we were about to board the newest attraction at Disneyland.

"Good morning!" Mike said cheerily, handing the officer our computer printouts with seat assignments.

"Your IDs?" he answered, nodding to me and Mike.

"Here you go," we said in unison, handing over our respective driver's licenses.

"And how old are you kids?"

"Eight," said Gabriella.

"Almost nine," said Jacob.

"Jacob and Gideon," the agent read on the tickets. "You two can keep your sneakers on when you walk through security. Parents, you'll need to take off your shoes."

"Great, thanks, sir." I nodded. "Have a great day. Let's go, kiddos."

I'm pretty sure Mike and the whole airport heard my audible sigh of relief.

"He didn't even ask who was who!" I said to Mike as we made our way toward the box of bins placed in front of the screening machines.

The kids walked through the explosive detector first. Mike and I followed. There was no buzz and no further questions.

"I knew it would be okay," Mike whispered to me with a smile.

"Well, I'm not sure we'll always be that lucky," I said tersely.

With years of this ahead of me, I was going to need to learn new coping skills. Or at least learn to bring a fresh shirt to change into on the plane.

24: Does This Dress Make My Penis Look Big?

Within one week of beginning my job doing local TV news at the CBS affiliate in Kansas, I found myself interviewing the late Fred Phelps, founder of the very much still alive Westboro Baptist Church. Renowned for their anti-gay picketing at military funerals and everyday events, Fred and his followers (mostly his family—go figure) carried signs with slogans like "God Hates Fags." Fast-forward twenty-five years, and church members have expanded their targets to include the transgender community and any organization, school, or group that promotes trans rights.

I totally understand that the Westboro Baptist Church is little more than a fringe group of crazed fanatics. And some of my friends who've been the most supportive of G's transition are people I met in Kansas. But I also know it's generally easier to pull aside a random store owner to explain that my daughter is trans and we might need some extra help finding clothes that cover certain parts of her body in Manhattan, New York, than it is in Manhattan, Kansas.

Easier doesn't mean *easy*, however. And I was quickly learning that nothing about getting dressed was easy for my daughter, even when she "loved" the outfit in question.

She'd been eyeing the dress in the window for weeks. And when she finally tried it on—a spaghetti-strapped yet totally age-appropriate, whimsical number with an abstract pattern of summer pinks, blues, and oranges on a white backdrop—her smile said it all. And after we paired it with the distressed, cropped jean jacket I found on an adjacent rack, she practically danced out of the store in her new outfit.

Gabby and her new sundress seemed to glide down the few blocks leading to the nail salon, where she picked out a sparkly pink polish that complemented her new look. And she seemed super happy as we sat next to each other getting our mommy-daughter manicures.

Maybe that's why I was surprised, disappointed, and yes, slightly devastated when, three days later, she ripped off the dress and threw it in a ball on the floor a few minutes before we were supposed to leave for school.

"What's the matter?" I asked. "You love that dress! And you look beautiful in it!"

"You can see my penis," she groaned. "I can't wear it."

"Babe, you can't see your penis at all."

"You're just saying that because you're my mother."

Honestly, that wasn't the case. You couldn't see her penis. Period. Well, maybe a *little* if she lay on the ground and spread her legs into some position I couldn't imagine her contorting into at any school-sanctioned activity, but which she proceeded to show me anyway. And once she did, despite my pleading, she wouldn't budge; she was convinced there was a bulge. She left her favorite dress in her room and threw on a pair of jean shorts and a T-shirt, and together we walked to school. She might have smiled at some point along the way. But if so, it was only slight. And it certainly didn't last long.

The reality? Even after socially transitioning, there were still limitations to what she could wear, unless she wanted to risk questions or stares at best, potential harassment (or worse) at worst. And it was those worst-case scenarios that often kept me awake at night.

‡ ‡

In November of 2017, the Human Rights Coalition and Foundation and the Trans People of Color Coalition released the *Time to Act:*

Fatal Violence Against Transgender People in America in 2017 report, documenting the heartbreaking, and often deadly, violence perpetrated on the trans community. A record twenty-nine transgender people were murdered in America in 2017, with trans women of color disproportionately victimized.[1] While I didn't worry about Gabriella becoming a target of violence at eight years old, I most certainly worried about bullying. And the report painted a disturbing picture on that front as well: "Since the election of Donald Trump, there has been a notable increase in the vitriol and anti-Transgender rhetoric—from top levels of government down through the rest of American society. Seventy percent of respondents to HRC's post-election 2016 youth survey reported witnessing bullying and harassment during and after the 2016 election, and almost half of LGBTQ youth said they have taken steps to hide who they are since the election."[2]

I didn't blame Trump for my daughter's desire to hide her penis, but I did blame him for enabling those who would want to harm my daughter or any other trans child or adult. Truth be told, Gabriella didn't yet understand that her gender identity immediately made her a target in some circles, largely because we didn't feel it was appropriate to tell an eight-year-old that. She did understand, however, that she couldn't always dress like the typical girls in her circle.

Leggings. That's what most of her peers wore. Seems easy, right? And it was, for her girlfriends without a penis. But G wearing leggings required our investing in lots of longer T-shirts and sweaters. She would have liked nothing better than to wear the belly shirts some of her friends favored, but she understood—mostly—that this style didn't work for her. (Honestly, I'm not sure the style works for any third grader, but that's a separate issue.)

The fact of the matter was, my daughter was a beautiful girl. One with a gorgeous body. A body that just so happened to have a penis.

Which we could really minimize in the fall, winter, and spring. But in summer?

I remembered running around our local swim club in bikinis when I was a little girl. When I was an even littler girl, I didn't even bother wearing the top. What for? My chest looked like every other kid's at the club.

But I wasn't worried about the bikini top. It was the bikini bottom that scared me.

To be fair, many summer camps, even some country clubs, had banned bikinis for girls. No need to oversexualize kids; that was apparently the thought behind the move. But for G, even a one-piece came with one big problem.

Enter the swim skirt.

‡ ‡

Traditionally favored mostly by middle-aged moms and the residents of almost every fifty-five-and-over community in South Florida, the swim skirt is a trans girl's best friend/worst enemy.

"Why do I need to wear the skirt?" my daughter asked as she got dressed the first morning of our first warm-weather getaway since her transition. "It keeps falling off."

Which was true, even when she cinched it with a hair band.

"Nobody will notice my penis," said the same kid who worried about the nonexistent bulge in her sundress.

"Love, please wear the skirt," I pleaded. "It's safer."

"What do you mean 'safer'?"

I knew what I meant. But instead of telling her, I just said, "Because you don't want anyone looking at you funny or asking you questions about your body." I wanted to add, "And every time you get out of a pool, your penis goes 'boing!'" but decided that when it comes to some topics, less is more.

She hated her swim skirts. I'm not sure I blamed her. I was forty-seven and I still wore a bikini. (And would as long as I could pull one off.) She was nine years old. She wanted to look like the other girls.

"But, Mommy, no one wears these!" she continued complaining as we walked toward the pool.

"I'm sorry that you hate the swim skirts so much," I said, and I meant it. But there wasn't much more I could say.

I decided these were the times I needed to listen and not try to fix things. To *not* try to change her mind. To *not* try to convince her that she looked adorable. These were the times I needed to *hear* her, really hear what she was saying, and try to imagine how I might feel if I were her and couldn't wear the same piece of clothing that all of my friends wore.

I'm pretty sure I'd feel how she felt. Sad. Angry. Like life was unfair.

As her mom, I hated that G had to worry so much about what she wore, that she had to make sure to cover the parts she wished she didn't have. I also felt guilty. As though it was my fault that my daughter was born with a penis. Like I was somehow to blame. That my husband and I—but mostly I—had failed her by birthing a child whose outsides largely betrayed her insides.

Thankfully she seemed to forget about the swim skirt once we got to the pool. Probably because we just happened to bump into one of her new friends from her new school. A girl who didn't know G was trans and who—get this—was wearing a swim skirt . . . by choice!

"Eva!" G screamed when she saw her sitting with her parents at the corner of the pool.

The two girls ran toward each other and hugged like it had been two months, not two days, since they'd last seen each other.

G and her pal spent that day jumping and splashing in the various pools while Eva's mom, Deb, and I sipped cocktails, swam with the kids, and laughed at our good fortune of randomly finding each other a couple thousand miles from the city.

"You know I cringe every time my daughter puts on a bathing suit, right?" I confided to Eva's mom as we dangled our feet in the pool, sipped margaritas, and watched the girls take turns doing somersaults and flips in the water.

"She looks adorable," Deb said.

"I know," I agreed, "but"—I dropped my voice to a whisper—"I get so scared someone will notice her penis."

"I was talking to my husband about Gabby earlier by the pool," Deb admitted, taking in the sun and an extra-large gulp of her margarita. "He said you and Mike are rock stars. He also said he's not sure how he'd react if one of our kids was trans."

"He'd deal," I said. "He'd have no other choice."

"Maybe. But the reality is, we'll probably never know."

"Ladies, another round?" a poolside waiter asked as he approached us and noticed our margarita levels running low.

"We probably shouldn't," we both said in unison and laughed.

"Which means we will," I said to Deb and the waiter. "One more round; this one's on me."

‡ ‡

The second morning at the resort, Mike, Jacob, Gabriella, and I headed to the pool to lay out our beach towels and "claim" our lounge chairs early. It was quiet; most people were either sleeping or eating breakfast. I breathed in the ocean air, looked out at the water, and smiled. I could tell we were going to have another warm, sunny day.

We were headed back toward the buffet in the main building when I noticed it. A small pile of purple-and-pink material wadded up on the ground, next to the waterslide.

No way, I thought as I walked over to pick it up.

Yup, it was Gabriella's swim skirt. She'd apparently taken it off the day before, and either nobody had noticed—her dad and I included— or no one had said anything.

‡ ‡

Trans kids can grow or chop their hair; they can start wearing skirts instead of cargo shorts (or vice versa). But there are still certain physical differences that can be difficult, if not impossible, to ignore.

And while many trans teens take puberty blockers to put the pause on puberty, you can't simply erase a penis or stomp out breast buds.

I knew a mom whose seventeen-year-old AFAB child had recently told her she was planning to transition. It turned out that she had been secretly binding her boobs for years.

Another mom friend of mine had an AMAB daughter who competed on the swim team. I remembered speaking to her a few days before her first swim meet as a girl. She was petrified; her daughter was well endowed, and she worried that fans would focus on her penis, not her performance.

Apparently, the mom's fears were unfounded. While she was busy concentrating on her kid's appendage, the judges, her teammates, and the fans were focused on her stellar speed in the pool.

Perhaps we moms and dads are projecting our panic on our trans kids? Is it possible that no one else notices that the AFAB boy has a curvier bottom half than that of his cisgender guy friend? Or that the AMAB girl's breast buds are nonexistent while some of her closest girlfriends are beginning to develop?

It's possible.

These days, with a few years to go before puberty, I was more concerned about Gabriella's emotional well-being. As "one of the girls," she wanted to dress like the other girls. Yet often she grew sad, angry, and/or frustrated when it came time to get dressed.

Mike didn't fully understand how or why it was so tough.

"Why don't we just buy ten pairs of the leggings she likes and multiple versions, in varying colors, of the shirts she wears most?" he asked me repeatedly.

"I'm trying to do that, Mike, but it's hard!" I'd shake my head. "She barely likes any of the tops we find. And when she does settle on one, it's often the *only* one. It's not like a Fruit of the Loom T-shirt or pocket tee that you can pick up in fifteen colors."

"Still," he'd say, "the kids are supposed to put out their clothes for the next morning the night before they go to bed. That's part of their jobs." We'd printed out the kids' list of jobs and hung them in their room so there'd be no ambiguity. "There should be no guesswork in the morning. All she needs to do is put on the outfit she already chose."

"*In theory*, you're right," I agreed. "But when she gets dressed in the morning and looks in the mirror, she often doesn't like what she sees."

"Again," he insisted, "that's why we have the kids put out their clothes at night. So they can't change their minds."

I could feel my face getting hot. "I get it, Mike. I do. But I don't think she's just changing her mind to be difficult. I think she's changing it because she doesn't think she looks like the other girls, and that makes her sad. And to be honest, that breaks my heart."

"I don't think she dresses differently than the other girls."

"But *she* thinks she does, Mike. And that's what matters. Besides, sometimes she really does have to dress different. Just look at gymnastics class!"

Did I mention my daughter's new favorite sport was gymnastics? (Of course it was.) And did I mention that for a girl taking lessons for the first time, she was really good? (Of course she was.)

Cute gym shorts over cute leotard. That's how we were handling gymnastics for now. If she went to the Olympics one day—her new goal, which I was reluctant to squash—I was sure the uniform would be the least of our concerns.

‡ ‡

The good news? I was learning more every day about strategies and even clothing lines designed specifically to help trans kids and adults fit in . . . literally. The bad news? None of them sounded particularly comfortable to me; some seemed downright painful.

Take "tucking," for instance. The Transgender Care unit at the University of California San Francisco Medical Center explains "tucking" on its website: "Tucking allows a visibly smooth crotch contour. In this practice, the testicles (if present) are moved into the inguinal canal, and . . . the penis and scrotum [are situated] posteriorly in the perineal region. Tight fitting underwear, or a special undergarment known as a gaffe is then worn to maintain this alignment. In some cases, adhesive or even duct tape may be used. In addition to local skin effects, this practice could result in urinary trauma or infections, as well as testicular complaints, which are covered elsewhere."[3]

Tucking had been around for ages. But in no world could I imagine my nine-year-old daughter positioning her penis that way, let alone duct taping it; the thought alone made me cry.

Which is why I was thrilled to learn about LeoLines underwear and even more thrilled to read a review on Etsy, where a trans woman declared them "a lifesaver." Another wrote, "No more secret tucking techniques that may cause discomfort or mobility issues. Overall gender euphoria."[4]

Described as "Transgender MTF concealing underwear," each pair featured padded panels sewn into the front designed to flatten and hide the penis. There were lots of pretty patterns and styles to choose from, which made me even more hopeful.

When I told Gabriella about the underwear, she was over the moon.

"Yay!" she exclaimed. "Now I can wear what all my other friends wear!"

She was less excited to learn that they were custom made and she'd need to wait a couple of weeks to receive them. But when the FedEx packages did arrive, she was all smiles. And when she walked to school the next day wearing leggings and a shirt that fell just below her waist but above her penis, she was the picture of happiness and confidence.

‡ ‡

Fast-forward three weeks and Gabriella's teachers, who were completely in the dark about her new underwear, called to let us know about Gabriella's new bathroom habits. Apparently, she'd been visiting the restroom more frequently (about three times as often, according to their tabulations), and they wanted to make sure everything was okay. Turned out the underwear weren't as comfortable as our daughter had led us to believe, and she admitted she'd been rushing to the restroom to adjust herself multiple times a day.

Gabriella stopped wearing her new underwear shortly thereafter. In retrospect, I'm surprised she lasted as long as she did . . . she was still a sensory kid. How could anyone expect such a kid to intentionally squash her balls and penis for a prolonged period of time—or *any* time, really?

I knew my daughter was still finding her sense of style—figuring out what she liked, what she didn't, and what worked for her fashion-wise and body-wise. I also knew that I sometimes cared more about what she wore than she or the rest of the world did.

I sincerely hoped, and mostly believed, that with time I'd chill out and take a less active role in Gabby's clothing choices, and she would grow more confident making her own decisions. But for now, I still found myself muttering, "Please, dear God, let her wear the skirt that goes with that bikini," every time we headed to a pool.

25: Odd Man Out

As Gabby struggled to fit into her underwear, Jacob struggled to fit in—with his friends, our family, and his preconceived notion of what his life was supposed to look like. From my perspective, it wasn't just being the odd man out; Jacob seemed to feel *put* out by his sister's transition. Sometimes literally.

"How come I have to go to a therapist that's so far away?" he asked us almost every week. "I'm not the one who's transgender. Why do I need to go to that place?"

"That place" was the child study center downtown, where Gabriella saw her gender therapist and Jacob saw his new therapist. Now, instead of the two blocks and four minutes it had formerly taken Jacob to walk to his old feelings doctor, he had to make the same forty-minute, three-subway, crosstown/downtown trek G did. To be fair, we'd searched for a new therapist closer to home, but apparently there's not a plethora of people specializing in the treatment of the cisgender twin of a transgender sister—and in the absence of that, we thought it smart for Jacob to see someone in the same practice as G's therapist, so they could share information as needed.

Jacob was less concerned with our reasoning and more annoyed by this latest *inconvenience* "caused by his sister." And the list of inconveniences and perceived inequities seemed to be growing.

"Mom, everyone keeps asking me questions about Gabriella. It's so annoying!"

"Why does she still get invited to the birthday parties of my friends? She doesn't even go to their school anymore!"

"How come she gets to buy new clothes like every day? Shouldn't I get something?"

Mike and I knew we overcompensated when it came to G and clothes. Since she couldn't wear certain items the rest of the girls wore, we tried to "make up" for the loss by buying her more outfits—sometimes at prices we normally wouldn't consider—that she *could* wear. Occasionally, we'd ask Jacob if he wanted to go shopping too, but clothes didn't interest him. Seeing that his sister was receiving "more," though, upset him. I'm not sure I understood how much at the time.

We knew Jacob felt a mix of sadness, loss, and even confusion over G's transition. We tried our best to address his needs, but I'll always feel like we didn't do enough, know enough, or understand enough. I could (maybe even *should*) find solace knowing that resources in this area are still hard to come by, and that, to date, there have been very few studies examining the impact of having a trans sibling, especially among kids.

One study published in Australia in 2020 did find "siblings (ages 12–17) reported mixed experiences within the same family, with some struggling to adapt." Some siblings admitted they were worried about "being shamed" by their peers, and 75 percent reported episodes of discrimination or microaggression.[1]

But this study was admittedly small. And included only thirty-five family members of nine young people experiencing gender dysphoria.

I have found no studies including transgender twins.

From the get-go, Mike and I learned we were entering new parenting territory, not only when it came to G but also when it came to Jacob.

‡ ‡

I remember paying a shiva call with Jacob in the first few months after his sister transitioned. The father of one of his friends had passed away, and I drove us to a relative's home the night after the funeral. I was speaking to the friend's mom when I overheard his buddy Nate saying, "I think I liked your sister better when he was a boy."

I couldn't make out what Jacob said in return. I did inquire on our ride home, but all he would say was "I don't want to talk about it, Mom."

I let it go. But I wondered what it must have felt like for Jacob to hear those words from his friend. I still wonder.

Occasionally Jacob would "let me in," open up, and share how he was feeling.

"Mommy, do you miss Gideon?" he asked one night after I tucked him into bed, his sister already asleep one room away.

"I'm glad Gabriella is happy," I answered honestly, though dodging my son's actual question. "Do you miss Gideon?"

"I miss how things used to be," he said.

"What do you miss, love?"

"I miss having a twin brother. I miss playing soccer with Gideon."

"Gideon hated playing soccer, you know that!" I almost blurted out, but instead bit my tongue.

"I miss having a normal family," he added quietly.

And that's what hit home. Even my own son—now *my only son*—didn't think we had a normal family.

"What makes you think we don't have a normal family?" I asked.

"Come on, Mom," Jacob replied with a maturity well beyond his nine years, "how many families have a transgender kid?"

"It might not be the norm," I said matter-of-factly, "but it doesn't mean we're not a normal family."

"Whatever, Mom."

I wasn't sure even I believed what I was saying.

‡ ‡

A few days later, I got a text from a mom of one of Jacob's classmates—someone I didn't know well but liked a lot.

S: Hey! I have a great Jacob story to share. Do you have a minute?
Me: Of course. Will call in a sec.

It turned out it *was* a great story. Nothing monumental, but meaningful nonetheless. Jacob and Allie were in science class, the mom explained, when one of the boys—one of Jacob's friends—made fun of her for being little. (Allie is the smallest girl in the grade.) Jacob, the tallest in the grade, overheard and called out his buddy for being rude in front of the whole class and explained that people can't control how short or tall they are . . . and that it's mean to make fun of someone for that. After the bell rang and everyone was getting ready to switch classes, Jacob walked up to Allie and asked if she was okay.

I thanked the mom for sharing.

"Your son is a really kind kid," she said, "and a great ally."

Not sure if her choice of the word "ally" was symbolic, but I sort of hoped it was.

‡ ‡

"When one person transitions, the whole family transitions along with them."

That's what Jean Malpas at GFP always told us at our support groups. And I know he was right. Our whole family changed the moment G declared herself a transister. And while it was difficult for all of us, I don't think I'll ever fully comprehend how tough it was . . . how tough it *still is* . . . for Jacob.

26: Come One, Come All!

"You do realize Gabriella's gonna flip out when we tell her she's going to sleepaway camp, right?" I said to Mike one frigid afternoon in early winter.

"And that's why we're not telling her until we have to," Mike said.

"You don't think she'll be the least bit suspicious when a random camp director shows up at our apartment in half an hour?"

"Summer is still months away; we'll tell her we're just looking at potential options," he replied. "Which is true. We haven't locked in anything."

"Yet," I reminded him.

"Katie, let's just give it a chance, okay?"

"Okay. Maybe she'll think the camp sounds great."

"Exactly."

We'd reached out to a bunch of sleepaway camps for Gabby. I hadn't heard back from some; most of the others had admitted they "weren't sure they were prepared" for a trans camper.

"Do we tell the whole bunk someone in their group is trans?"

"Would we need to ask the other parents if they were okay with a transgender camper in their kids' bunk?"

"Where would your child change?"

These were just some of the questions camp directors asked me and Mike.

In fact, the only camp I'd reached out to that didn't bat an eye was the one suggested by the guy we'd met at one of those "rookie days" the previous summer. And today, the director of that camp was visiting our home.

"Be You, Boldly." That was the camp's tagline, which immediately jumped out at me when I clicked on the camp's website. That and the flagpole in the middle of camp, which was simultaneously flying American, Israeli, and LGBTQ Pride flags.

"We want you to be you," it said on the home page, which also claimed that at their camp, "there's never a reason for campers to be anyone other than their true selves. No matter who they are, our kids are both celebrated and challenged in ways that help them grow into amazing human beings."

That sounded good to us. Because obviously we wanted Gabriella—and Jacob too—to be their "true selves." And what better place to do that than at camp? Certainly, I hoped our kids could be and would be themselves everywhere. But I also recognized that for many kids, going to sleepaway camp—where they were far away from family and the friends they'd known for years—was an opportunity for a fresh start, a chance to rediscover themselves and be the person they really were (or, in some cases, to reinvent themselves and become the person they wanted to be).

For some transgender kids, I learned, "being themselves" meant going to exclusively transgender camps, of which there actually were a few. We thought about sending Gabriella to such a camp, even spoke to the founder of one. But G didn't want to be thought of as a trans-gender girl; she just wanted to be a girl.

I understood where she was coming from. I also understood it was difficult to find a "regular" camp that would accept a transgender camper. Other moms in my support groups had told me stories of sending their kids to camps that claimed to be supportive, only to find their child was made fun of for being trans. One boy was even asked to leave the cabin while his bunkmates were changing.

A quick look at this camp's website and a brief chat with its director confirmed that neither of these things would happen to our daughter if we sent her there. Immediately, I elevated it to "strong contender" status.

‡ ‡

The at-home visit sealed the deal.

"So, what do you like to do for fun?" Sari asked our daughter as Gabriella cartwheeled through our living room.

"Gymnastics. Art. Stuff."

"What kind of stuff?"

"Swimming, playing with my friends. Stuff like that."

"Well, we've got stuff like that," Sari told her.

"Yeah, but I bet your camp has bugs too."

"What's wrong with bugs?"

"I HATE bugs," G practically screamed before hopping off the couch and doing a handstand for forty-six seconds.

"Yeah, I'm not a fan either," Sari admitted. And then, "Impressive handstand."

The two bantered back and forth for a few minutes; then G said, "Your camp sounds cool. Can I go now, Mom?"

"Yes, Gabriella." I laughed. "Why don't you go finish your home-work, okay?"

"Okay." She started walking away, but then she turned back to Sari and singsonged, "Byy-eeee."

"She's one happy kid," Sari said to us when Gabriella closed the door to her room.

"Yeah, she is pretty happy," I agreed. "*When* she's happy." And then, "And you're sure the other thing won't be a big deal?"

"Positive. There are always a half dozen or so kids who come to camp with pull-ups," she assured us. "Not a big deal. We're on it."

"Pull-ups and a penis," I reminded her.

"We got you covered," she replied.

As if it wouldn't be challenging enough for our daughter to hide her penis at camp, she was also planning to hide her pull-ups. Our pediatrician said it was completely normal that an eight-and-a-half-year-old still occasionally wet the bed at night, that it had nothing to do with being transgender, and that a certain percentage of kids have bladders that simply take a while to mature. I just wished Gabriella wasn't one of those kids.

"Well, Sari, we can't thank you enough for coming to meet with us," Mike said. "We really appreciate it."

"My pleasure. Gabriella is clearly an awesome kid, and I'm sure she'll have a great summer."

"I hope you're right. I really think you're right," I said. "I mean, it still makes me nervous to send her. But Christ, if I could figure out a way to go back to camp myself, I'd go in a heartbeat!"

Mike laughed. "She really would, Sari. Kate's not kidding."

"I'm not kidding," I said as I walked Sari out, thanked her again, shut the door, and smiled to myself.

‡ ‡

Of all the camps we looked at, I have to say the Jewish ones—the Reconstructionist and Reform ones, especially—were the most welcoming to trans kids. My best friend in California (the mom of not–Jack Ashe) said the same thing. (Jared's camp was also run by the Reform movement.)

"It's kind of like 'come one, come all,'" I said to Mike one day. "Because of the Holocaust, Jews know what it's like to lose people. And now they welcome anyone who is nice, ready, willing, and able to join them. At least in *our* Jewish circle, you know?"

"I'm not sure that's *quite* it," he said. "But I'm glad our Jewish crew has been overwhelmingly supportive."

A quick look back at recent Jewish history gave me even better perspective. As early as 1965, the Women of Reform Judaism demanded homosexuality be decriminalized. In 1984, the Reconstructionist

Rabbinical College voted to accept and ordain rabbis regardless of sexual orientation, and just three years later, The Hebrew Union College Institute of Religion (the seminary of the Reform movement) changed its admission requirements to allow gay and lesbian students to join the school. Fast-forward to 2003 and they accepted Rueben Zellman, its first transgender applicant, who was ordained in 2010.[1]

Even more encouraging to me is the "Resolution on the Rights of Transgender and Gender Non-conforming People," which was officially adopted by the Union of Reform Judaism in November 2015.

Among the highlights of the resolution, the Union for Reform Judaism "affirms its commitment to the full equality, inclusion and acceptance of people of all gender identities and gender expressions" and "affirms the right of transgender and gender non-conforming individuals to be referred to by their name, gender, and pronoun of preference in our congregations, camps, schools, and other Reform affiliated organizations."[2]

In contrast, the Orthodox Jewish community has been far less supportive of transgender rights. I remember driving through an ultra-Orthodox neighborhood in Brooklyn shortly after Gabriella's transition and wondering what it must be like for members of that community who felt like they were born in the wrong body. Surely, there had to be some gender-nonconforming people among the long coats and beards, long skirts, and wigs, right?

Half of Mike's family was Orthodox, and while we knew of at least one distant relative who was gay, no one had ever mentioned the G word in front of us. I wondered if having a transgender child would be too much for them to handle; would our daughter be welcomed at future family functions?

Orthodox tradition is religiously organized and socially structured by biblical and rabbinic teachings with fixed gender roles. Practically speaking, that means the community is largely binary, with separate religious duties for men and women and separate spaces for them during worship. When it comes to LGBTQ inclusion, Orthodox policies are purportedly based on the Torah and subsequent rabbinic teachings that prohibit sexual relations between people of the same gender; further, Orthodoxy bases gender roles on birth biology, or what LGBTQ folks and allies refer to as "gender assigned at birth." Sex between men, particularly anal intercourse, is considered taboo, a violation of the bible. Interestingly, the bible doesn't specifically mention lesbians, but it seems Orthodox rabbinic authorities prohibit sexual relationships between women regardless of Torah statute.

That said, it's important to note that no sect of Judaism, Orthodox included, is one-size-fits-all. Some Orthodox congregations—even some Orthodox rabbis—may be personally welcoming to LGBTQ congregants. In 2010, more than 150 Orthodox rabbis and educators made the unprecedented move of signing a declaration calling for the welcoming of LGBTQ Jews into their community.[3] Still, it can be difficult, if not impossible, for most transgender people to navigate Orthodox communities, in part because gender reassignment surgery is forbidden in Jewish law, based on a law against male castration.[4]

Again, there are anomalies and exceptions. Take Abby Stein, for instance. She came out as transgender in 2015, three years after she received her rabbinical degree from an ultra-Orthodox Hasidic school, thereby becoming the first openly trans woman to be ordained by an Orthodox institution.[5]

Then again, she is no longer a practicing rabbi.

Luckily, my kid didn't want to be an Orthodox rabbi; she only wanted to go to sleepaway camp. (Well, *we* wanted our daughter to go to sleepaway camp.) What's more, it looked like we now had an incredible option.

An hour after Sari left our apartment, our doorman buzzed up. Our dinner delivery had arrived. Chinese takeout—Gabriella's favorite.

"Kiddos," I yelled across the living room, "dinner is here! Come one, come all!"

27: "You Mean My Sister"

I've never thought of myself as the military type. I'm not good at following orders, I don't often agree with our nation's wartime policies, and as a former TV news reporter, I can't stand the official language members of the military use when responding to interview questions. ("Sergeant, can you please re-answer that question in layman's terms?" I asked more than a handful of times while holding a microphone at Fort Riley or Fort Dix.) But I've always respected people who choose to join the military, and routinely thank the servicemen and women I encounter, particularly since 9/11. And while I don't expect either of my kids will ever join the army, it stung—big time—when on March 24, 2018, the White House followed through on Trump's controversial policy pledge and announced orders to formally ban transgender people from serving in the military.[1]

Never mind that the order came despite opposition from top military leaders and previous rulings against the ban, which various LGBTQ groups had challenged in court. What mattered to me was that this once theoretical policy—applauded primarily by those I would describe as homophobic and transphobic—was now the official law of the land. And the people credited with moving the dial weren't some random fringe groups; the White House maintained the policy was "developed through extensive study by senior uniformed and civilian leaders" and based on the advice of "experts."

And what, exactly, did these so-called experts from the Trump administration conclude? That the "accession or retention" of trans people "presents considerable risk to military effectiveness and lethality."[2]

"It's not the trans community that poses the risk to the military," I said to Mike one night as we lay in bed watching Rachel Maddow break down the ban. "It's Trump and his cronies who are threatening the trans community!"

Mike nodded.

We were both becoming increasingly worried. Not for our daughter, per se—she was about as likely to join the military as Trump ever was—but about the general anti-trans sentiment we could feel boiling over in parts of our country.

"I think it's time we change Gabriella's name," I blurted out during a commercial break. "Like, officially change it. On her birth certificate."

"I've been thinking the same thing," Mike agreed.

"I'm scared if we don't do it soon, the laws could change. I mean, what'll happen if Gabriella *can't* change her name?"

"That's not gonna happen," he assured me. "But we should still get on it."

Which is how we found ourselves surfing the Internet the following morning and scanning the "About" section of Transcend Legal's website:

Vision: A world in which all people—transgender and cisgender— are equally recognized, respected and celebrated.

Purpose: Transcend Legal cultivates equitable social, medical and legal recognition of transgender people by offering culturally competent, transgender-led legal representation, public policy advocacy, community empowerment, and public education.

Among Transcend's specialty areas? New York name changes and transgender health insurance.

Clearly, we'd stumbled upon the right place.

‡ ‡

Two weeks later, Mike and I secured a meeting with Transcend's founding attorney, who gave us the lowdown on the name-change process.

"You and Gabriella will need to go before a judge," he explained.

"Will Gabriella need to testify?" I asked.

"She'll need to be in the courtroom, and she'll need to answer some questions," he told us. "But more likely than not, the judge will escort her and the two of you to a separate room, where he or she will talk with all of you in private."

"Do the judges usually grant the name changes?" Mike wanted to know.

"I've never seen a New York City judge *not* grant a name and gender change," he said. "If all goes as planned, Gabriella will get a new birth certificate, with her new name and gender marker."

"So, her new birth certificate will say she's a girl? Not a trans girl?" I asked.

"Exactly. She'll be recognized by the government as female."

"Wow" was all I could think to say.

I squeezed Mike's hand and turned to face him. He was wiping away tears.

"Are you okay?" I asked.

He nodded, then started asking questions, rapid-fire: "How long does this process take? When do we go in front of the judge? What happens to her old birth certificate? How do we get a new birth certificate?"

Our attorney laid it all out for us calmly, warmly, and quite clearly from a place of care and experience. (He, too, was trans and had already gone through the name-change process for himself, as well as represented dozens of people through it all.) Most of what he told us seemed simple enough—except the publicity part. Apparently, when a trans person legally changes their name, they need to publish an advertisement in a newspaper announcing the change.

"Are you serious?" I asked.

"Unfortunately, I am," he said.

"So, essentially, we need to 'out' our stealth daughter in order for her to effectively stay stealth?"

He agreed the notion was unfair, bordering on ridiculous, and explained our options: We could have the announcement placed in a small periodical, one with little circulation and little likelihood that anyone, let alone anyone we knew, would read the article. Or we could petition the court to waive the publication provision.

To me and Mike, the decision was a no-brainer. And we soon discovered we were not the first people (or parents) to object to these "forced outings."

In November of 2009, the National Center for Transgender Equality blogged:

Governments force transgender people to disclose that they are transgender all the time. They make us carry around little pieces of paper and plastic with our birth-assigned sex listed on them, just begging any police officer, bank teller, customs official, airline agent or the like to ask just what are you anyway? They keep that old sex designation in computer files—your driving record, your Social Security record, Medicare record—that get shared here and there. They make us appear in open court, or take out an ad in the newspaper, to announce that we're changing our name from Kate to Kevin, or from Kevin to Kate. They say this is necessary for "accuracy" and "fraud prevention." These government systems very seldom recognize the very real dangers of the official outing of trans people in so many areas of our lives—the dangers not only of embarrassment, discrimination and harassment, but the very real danger of violence when we are outed against our will to untold numbers of strangers.[3]

Historically, petitioners in New York were only granted exceptions to the "newspaper rule" if they were the victims of domestic violence and believed publicizing their name change would pose a threat to their safety. But in November 2009, a trans man challenged this premise. His lawyers stood before the Westchester Supreme Court and pointed to numerous reports indicating the high rates of bias-motivated violence against transgender people, as well as the Hate Crimes Prevention Act passed on October 22, 2009.

The presiding judge concluded that while the young man "did not, and hopefully could not, cite a personal experience of violence or crime against him based on his gender identity, he has made a compelling argument as to why, at the age of twenty, he has a right to feel threatened for his personal safety in the event his transgender status is made public." Accordingly, the judge granted the exemption, made the name change immediately, and ordered that the court records be sealed.[4]

While I was grateful for the precedent, I acknowledged the irony: State courts hear literally thousands of petitions for name changes each year; they grant most of them automatically and seldom render a written opinion. The obvious exception? When the person seeking to change their name is transgender.

We told our lawyer we'd like to petition the court to waive the newspaper article. He said he'd circle back with a court date and some forms for us to fill out, as well as instructions for the letter one of Gabriella's doctors needed to write on her behalf. We shook hands, thanked him, and walked him to the door of our building's common room to say our goodbyes.

Mike suggested we stay there for a few minutes to review the name-changing materials. But I think he just wanted to cry a little more before we headed up to our apartment.

"I don't know why this is so hard for me," he said, wiping his eyes.

"Probably because this is official," I said. It was an instinctive answer, but I quickly realized I was on to something.

This was the first time I'd seen Mike cry since Gabriella's big announcement a year earlier. It was as though the name change served as a trigger, signaling to my "spreadsheet man" that he needed to change a column he'd never dreamed of altering—a formerly fixed and codified column that now lacked the prescribed formula that kept the spreadsheet, and Mike's world, in order.

I held my husband tight and promised him, "It's gonna be all right, my love. Everything is gonna be all right."

‡ ‡

When we got upstairs, Jacob was playing Fortnite with his friend Sam. Our babysitter was still on the clock, so Mike and I felt comfortable yielding to our emotional exhaustion and crashing in our bedroom.

I'd been asleep for maybe two minutes when I heard a literal crash coming from the living room.

"The kitchen stool," I said, lifting my head reflexively and turning to Mike.

Jacob generally co-opted one of the stools from the breakfast bar when he played Fortnite, planting it in front of the flat screen and making it his unofficial gaming chair. His new habit of leaning back on his unofficial gaming chair occasionally resulted in a big bang.

I dragged myself off the bed, walked to the door, and poked my head through to the living room to see if Jacob and Sam were okay.

"Jacob, you in one piece, my love? That was a pretty loud crash."

"Yeah, Mom, I'm fine. Sorry about that."

Our sitter walked out of the hall bathroom, saw me, and asked, "What did I miss?"

"Just a near-fatal gaming accident." I laughed. "Everyone's fine."

"That's good," she said. "I just heard from Lizzie's nanny. I'll run out and get Gabriella."

"Sounds like a plan," I told her as I heard Sam ask, "Jacob, where is your brother anyway?"

"You mean my sister?" Jacob corrected him.

"Yeah."

"She's at a friend's house."

I walked in our room, took one look at Mike, and realized he'd heard the exchange.

"That's the first time I've heard Jacob advocate for Gabriella," he said softly. "He corrected Sam and called her his sister."

"I know it." I bit my lip, which had begun to quiver.

And for the second time in one day, I saw Mike's eyes well up with tears.

28: Soap on a Rope

"You doing okay?" I whispered as Mike, Gabriella, and I walked down the hallway of one of the leading pediatric endocrinology departments in the country, G and I clutching one another's hands.

"I guess so," she said.

We were on our way to her first endocrinologist appointment.

"This shouldn't take too long, Supes," Mike told her. "And then we'll both take you to school."

"Can we at least take a taxi to school?" she half whined, half asked.

"Of course," we said in unison.

"Why does everything have to be so far from our apartment?" she complained.

"Technically, this office is pretty close," I told her. "But I agree, it sure feels far away, especially during rush hour."

This new doc was just around the corner from Gabriella's gender therapist. Only 2.7 miles from our home, but downtown and across the park—pretty much Uganda in "city terms," especially when traveling with an anxious kid at 8:30 a.m. on a weekday. It had taken eight subway stops, three transfers, and a shoulder-to-shoulder walk/trot through Grand Central Station to make it there. Thank God our "subway exposure therapy" had finally proven successful and Gabriella could now ride the subway if not enthusiastically, at least uneventfully.

"Hi, I'm Doctor Vega," a young, beautiful woman with dark

brown, shoulder-length hair and a warm, genuine smile said as we approached her office. "So nice to meet you!"

"Hi," G said quietly, eyes down, unlike her usual boisterous self.

"Hi, I'm Kate, Gabriella's mom," I jumped in.

Mike kept it going. "And I'm Mike, Gabriella's dad. Nice to meet you too."

"Thanks for coming in today," Dr. Vega said.

I looked around before taking a seat. Pretty typical for an exam room: a medical table, a few chairs, a scale, blood pressure monitor, Formica counters and cabinet with a sink. *Nothing particularly remarkable here*, I thought.

"So, do you know why you're here today?" Dr. Vega asked.

"Kind of," Gabriella answered.

"Well, we did talk about it, right?" I said, giving my daughter's hand a squeeze. "Remember, hon, the puberty stuff?"

"Yeah," she mumbled.

"Well, how about we talk for a few minutes," Dr. Vega continued. "I'll ask you some questions and then tell you what's going to happen here today. Sound okay?"

"I guess."

"First of all, what grade are you in? Where do you go to school? And, most importantly, what are your favorite things to do inside and outside of school?"

"I'm in third grade," Gabriella told her, "and I really love my new school."

Gabriella began to loosen up—started talking about her friends, her favorite art class, gymnastics. Within a minute or two, I saw her shoulders relaxing; she even cracked a smile. The two bantered back and forth a bit more before Dr. Vega said she needed to give Gabriella a brief exam.

"I'm going to need to look at your private parts, Gabriella. Would you be more comfortable if I pull the curtain, so your parents can't see, or would you prefer I keep the curtain open?"

"Umm, you can keep it open," Gabriella replied softly.

"Remember, Gabriella," Mike interjected, "Dr. Vega is allowed to examine your privates because she's a doctor. We don't show our private parts to just anyone."

"I know, Dad," Gabriella said with a tinge of attitude. "I'm not stupid!"

Dr. Vega motioned to the exam table, and our daughter hopped on top. She asked Gabriella to lie on her back and pull down her pants a bit.

That's when I saw Dr. Vega reach for a small bag and pull out what I can only describe as the beaded version of "soap on a rope."

Holy throwback! I thought. My mom had given soap on a rope as gifts when I was a little girl. I'd always found them fascinating. They weren't your standard Ivory or Dial types but rather the fancy variety, often handcrafted and intricately molded into pretty shapes of different colors, resembling artwork more than a personal hygiene product. Sometimes my mom had used her own soaps on a rope as bathroom decor.

It wasn't until years later I'd learned the actual benefits of the stylish soap, which, much to my surprise, had nothing to do with prison. The idea was that washers could wear the ropes on their wrists to avoid dropping the soap on the shower floor; then they could use the rope to hang-dry the soap afterward, reducing the likelihood the soap would dissolve in a frequently water-soaked soap dish.

I was trying to imagine why on earth our doctor was holding this thing when I made two observations: (1) the beads were different sizes, and (2) Dr. Vega was starting to dangle the beads closer to my daughter's testicles.

No fucking way, I thought. *This is how they measure ball size? How archaic!*

I was seriously scared that I might burst out laughing.

I was also scared how Gabriella might react to a doctor comparing her balls to wooden beads.

Then my obsessive-compulsive side kicked in: *How do they wash the wooden beads between patients?* I wondered. *Oh my god, what if they* don't *wash the beads?*

Hearing Dr. Vega's words snapped me back into reality.

"So, Gabriella, I'm just taking a look at your testicles," she said. "And everything looks great."

I wasn't sure how anything about a girl with testicles could look great, but I knew what Dr. Vega meant.

"It doesn't look like you've started the puberty process," she continued, "so for now we just wait and see."

Phew. Gabriella still hadn't hit puberty. While this was the news we'd expected, I was still relieved. We didn't need to do anything medical yet. It would be about ten years before Gabriella could undergo sexual reassignment surgery, but puberty blockers could be anywhere from a few years to just a few months in our future.

Gabriella already knew she'd take puberty blockers once the first signs of puberty emerged—and the first signs, it turned out, were often testicle and penis growth, hence the soap-on-a-rope contraption. The puberty blockers would ensure Gabriella's "little-kid penis" didn't grow into a "big adult penis." Gabriella hated her penis to begin with, and the thought of it growing any bigger was pretty scary. That was where the puberty blockers came in.

In simple terms, puberty blockers put the pause on puberty. They do so by blocking estrogen and testosterone, the hormones that lead to puberty-related changes in the body. Puberty blockers come in two forms: a small rod-like implant called histrelin acetate that's placed under the skin and lasts for about a year, or a shot called leuprolide acetate, which must be administered by a doctor every one to four months.[1]

Historically, puberty blockers were used to treat a condition known as precocious puberty, the abnormally early onset of puberty. Why would anyone care if a kid hits puberty early? For a couple of reasons. The first are social and emotional: young girls and boys who begin puberty well before their peers can become very self-conscious about their bodies, often leading to depression or substance abuse. Second, precocious puberty can stunt a person's height. Kids with precocious puberty may grow faster at first and be taller than children their age, but they often stop growing before their peers.[2]

My friend's daughter began taking puberty blockers at the age of eight, when her parents noticed she was starting to develop breast buds and a few stray pubic hairs. Already concerned she'd be unusually small (my friend and her husband are both below average height), her parents took her to a specialist for a series of tests. A pediatric endocrinologist ultimately recommended puberty blockers to temporarily stave off her period and give her the chance to eke out a few more inches before she stopped growing. Fast-forward several years, and my friend's kiddo is five foot five, a talented high school soccer player, and, most importantly, a seemingly happy, well-adjusted teenager.

The stakes for trans kids who don't take puberty blockers can be much higher—so much so that guidelines from the Endocrine Society, the American Academy of Pediatrics, and the World Professional Association for Transgender Health recommend that transgender adolescents be offered blockers to suppress puberty. In 2020, a first-of-its-kind study found a link between puberty blockers and lower odds of suicidal thoughts. Researchers from Massachusetts General Hospital, Boston Children's Hospital, and the Fenway Institute analyzed the data from more than 20,000 transgender adults, ages 18–36, and found that "approximately 9 out of 10 transgender adults who had wanted but were denied pubertal suppression reported having suicidal ideation during their lifetime."[3]

This doesn't mean puberty blockers are a panacea. They can't guarantee a transgender person won't feel depressed, nor can they prevent puberty from beginning. They can, however, "pause" puberty once it begins. In practical terms, that would mean keeping Gabriella's genitals from growing big, her voice from deepening, her upper lip from sprouting a mustache, and an Adam's apple from forming.

Perhaps equally important? Puberty blockers help "buy time" for kids like Gabriella, allowing them to solidify their gender identity (a.k.a. ensure it's not just a phase) before they develop secondary sexual characteristics, without making any permanent changes to their bodies. If Gabriella later decided to detransition, she could simply stop taking the puberty-blocking meds, and her body would go through traditional male puberty. If she determined she was indeed trans, as I was 99.9999999999 percent sure she was, then when she was old enough, she could start taking female hormones and potentially consider gender reassignment surgery without having to worry about getting rid of excess facial hair or manly abs, making her transition into life as an adult woman that much easier.

So, yay! This was good news. Gabriella hadn't hit puberty yet, and she could spend the next months, or even years, without worrying about her body changing. For now, she could just be a pre-tween girl.

But Dr. Vega wasn't done yet.

"Let's plan to check in every six months, so we don't miss the onset of puberty," she said. Looking at me and Mike, she added, "Puberty is a pretty slow process. Nothing happens overnight. So, by meeting every six months, we'll be in a great position to pause things when we need to." She turned back to Gabriella. "And all you need to do, Gabriella, is to keep on doing what you're doing, 'cause you're doing awesome. Sound like a plan?"

"Yup." G nodded. "Sounds good to me."

"Great. Now a couple housekeeping things, Kate and Mike, before we go. Is Gabriella taking any medications right now?"

"Yes," we both answered.

"She takes some allergy stuff," I said. "Maybe Zyrtec and Allegra?"

"And Nasacort too," Mike added. "Gabriella's really sensitive to pollen."

"My eyes get all puffy and my nose won't stop running," Gabriella explained. "My face looks terrible!"

"Your face always looks beautiful," I tried to reassure her.

"You're just saying that 'cause you love me." She made a face at me.

"Oh," Mike jumped in, "she also takes Cotempla."

"Cotempla?" Dr. Vega asked. "What's that for?"

I shot Mike a look, but he didn't notice.

"ADHD," he explained.

"ADHD?" Gabriella repeated. And then she started crying. "I have ADHD?" she screamed.

Ugh. Not what we needed right now.

"Oh, babe." I gave her a big hug. "Millions of people have ADHD. I promise, it's not a big deal."

I looked at Mike again. He was biting his lip and looking at the ceiling. He knew he'd messed up. He'd been so insistent we not tell Gabriella she had ADHD that we'd been referring to her morning meds as "her vitamins" for the past year, explaining that the little white chewable pills helped her to focus better. Never mind that within the first month of switching to her new school G had reported that almost everyone in her class took "brain medication."

Our daughter was inconsolable.

"Why didn't you tell me I had ADHD?" she asked, the tears streaming down her cheeks at about the same rate as the boogers were running from her nose.

"Sweetie," I pleaded, "you're right, we should have told you earlier. But please believe me, tons of people have ADHD—everyday people, famous people—and it has nothing to do with how happy or successful you'll be."

"Do any gymnasts have ADHD?" she asked, wiping her nose with her sleeve.

"Not sure about gymnasts," I admitted. "But Michael Phelps, the greatest swimmer of all time—the one who won the most gold medals *ever* at the Olympics—has ADHD, and it sure didn't stop him!"

"Do you think Simone Biles has ADHD?" Gabriella asked. She was starting to calm down.

Dr. Vega remained patiently quiet.

"I honestly don't know about Simone Biles," I told her. "But I'm sure some gymnasts must have it."

A new doctor had just compared my daughter's balls to beads and discussed pausing puberty, and my kiddo had little to no reaction. But the mere mention that she had ADHD? Well, that had nearly sent her over the edge. Was she really that upset over the diagnosis? Or was it easier for her to get flustered over that than it was to consider why we were seeing an endocrinologist in the first place?

Consoling Gabriella about ADHD was certainly easier for me than thinking about the changes and challenges my kiddo would face when she finally entered puberty. Puberty can be brutal for most kids: mood swings, the appearance of body hair, and acne, among many other things. I couldn't fathom what it must be like for trans kids—and more specifically, my kid! Would Gabriella be jealous when her friends started developing breasts and her chest remained flat? Would the other kids make fun of her? And what about crushes? I had boyfriends in sixth and seventh grade. Would she? Would boys be scared to "like" her if they knew she was trans? Puberty blockers would ensure my daughter didn't grow an Adam's apple, but they couldn't protect her from bullies or people who might target her because she was trans.

I could envision what Jacob would look like when he hit puberty— his body filling out, his legs getting hairier and stronger, a little peach fuzz growing on his upper lip. But I had no idea what my daughter would look like when she finally went through puberty—presumably a few years after she went on the blockers and got the go-ahead to start taking female hormones. Would the shape of her face change? Would her body grow curves? Would she develop full breasts?

As happy as I was that Dr. Vega would help us through the first stages of this process, I hated that my daughter must go through it at all. I knew it was what she needed; I also knew it would be difficult. Lifesaving and potentially backbreaking (emotionally and, at times, physically) all at the same time. Up until now we had dealt solely with Gabriella's social transition. Meeting with Dr. Vega signaled the start of her medical/physical transition. So, yes, perseverating over my daughter's ADHD instead of her transition was likely less complicated, and therefore preferable, for all of us.

"Well, I think we have a great plan in place, Gabriella," Dr. Vega chimed in, breaking the silence. "And your parents are right. Millions of people have ADHD and there's nothing wrong with that. Why don't you guys head to the front desk and make an appointment for six months from now? And if you have any questions between now and then, Gabriella, I'm always here."

"Thanks again, Dr. Vega," I said. "We really appreciate your help."

"Yes, thanks," Mike said, trying to feign a smile but looking like he might throw up his last six months of meals.

‡ ‡

Gabriella didn't say much in the cab uptown.

"The subway would have been quicker," I whispered to Mike, hoping I'd get him to smile. But no such luck.

By the time we dropped G off at school, she seemed in slightly better spirits. We both kissed her goodbye, told her we loved her, and watched as she ran up the stairs toward her classroom.

"Holy fuck," I said as we walked outside and headed home. "What a morning."

"I can't believe I told her she has ADHD," Mike said.

"Mike, it's fine," I said, perhaps a little too harshly. And then, "Please don't be so hard on yourself. I honestly think it's best she knows. Granted, I wish she didn't find out this way, but it is what it is. Personally, I think we should have told her a long time ago."

"Maybe." Mike still sounded downcast. "But I'm sorry she had to find out like this."

"You do realize she's at a school where the kids learn to advocate for themselves and their learning differences, right?" I continued. "How can we expect her to advocate for her learning differences if she doesn't know what they are?"

"I know. But still," he lamented, "I feel terrible. I just wish things had gone differently."

"On a positive note, she doesn't have to deal with puberty blockers yet," I said. "That's good news, right?"

"I guess."

"Seriously, love, please give yourself a break. She's a strong girl. She's gonna be just fine."

29: Letting You Go

"Woohoo! That's what I'm talking about, J-man!" I screamed as I watched my son round first base and head toward second after slamming a line drive through the gap between left and center field. The kid was coming alive in the second half of the spring baseball season, and I couldn't be happier for him. He'd worked so hard to catch up to the other kids after his foot problems, and his determination was finally paying off.

But my favorite part of most games was watching him dance in between plays at first base. As much as he made fun of his sister for her love of TikTok, he had some moves of his own. And if there was a boom box in earshot, which was often the case at baseball fields in the city, watch out!

"Is the game almost over?" Gabriella groaned, oblivious to the excitement caused by Jacob's hit.

"Did you see your brother? He just got a double!"

"Yay, Jacob!" she screamed. "Great hit, number 9!"

I smiled. "That was really sweet of you."

"Thanks, I know." She smiled. "Can we go now?"

"Soon, baby girl, soon. The game is almost over. Then we'll snap a few family pics and get out of here."

"More pictures?" she asked, rolling her eyes. "Why?"

"So you and your bro have some recent pictures to put in your bunks this summer."

"I can't believe you're making me go to camp," she grumbled. Then she glanced at my iPhone, which I handed to her so she could record a new TikTok.

We'd let Gabriella know about camp one night in late April, after which she'd screamed and cried for a good twenty minutes. When she'd finally calmed down, we'd reminded her how much she'd liked meeting her camp's director and then sat with her while she watched several videos on the camp website. Then we'd told her Sari had sent us the names and numbers of some campers who lived near us, so Mike and I could arrange a few playdates/meetups before the summer started.

Now, in early June, Gabriella was starting to come around to the idea of camp. A bunch of her best friends would be trying sleepaway for the first time as well, and despite her clearly stated misgivings, she had to admit she was enjoying the shopping and other preparations leading up to the big day.

"Guys, just a couple more, okay? Big smiles!" I instructed as the parent of one of Jacob's teammates snapped a few of the four of us. "Thanks so much," I said as she handed me back the phone.

The kids hated when I asked them to pose for pictures. To be fair, I probably did ask more than most moms. But unlike most moms, I'd had to remove half of the pictures decorating the walls of our apartment when one of my sons became my daughter and asked that I excise any visible traces of "him" from our home. Pictures of our new family—with all four of us—were still a rare commodity, and I did want to make sure both kids could bring at least one picture of all of us to camp.

Part of me couldn't wait. I was exhausted. Emotionally, physically, mentally. The last eight months had pretty much kicked my ass. And I wanted—I *needed*—a reprieve. Some time for myself. Some time for me and Mike. Some time to do nothing. I also *needed* both kids to have a great summer. I wanted Jacob to get a fresh start, to go somewhere

where he was just "Jacob"—not a twin brother and definitely not the twin brother of a transgender sister. And I wanted Gabriella to feel safe, embraced, and liberated all at the same time.

‡ ‡

"Katie, the kids are both gonna be fine," Mike told me for about the thousandth time the week before they were scheduled to leave.

"I know," I said, "but I'm still scared! You do realize we're sending our daughter to camp with a penis and pull-ups?"

"She won't be the only one, Katie," he said patiently. "Sari already told us that."

"I guarantee she'll be the only girl with a penis wearing pull-ups," I shot back.

"Ha ha. You know that's not what I meant."

"I know." I paced the room. "But it's gonna be hard enough as it is for her to get dressed and undressed every day while trying to hide her penis. Now she has to hide her pull-ups too!"

"She'll do it, Katie. Sari promised the counselors would be on top of it."

"They better be." And then I got sort of excited. "Did I tell you I bought Gabriella this awesome tie-dye toiletry bag that she can carry with her to the bathroom every night and morning to hold her pull-ups and wipes? I can show it to you later."

"Cool," Mike said.

"The bag can hold a few nights' worth of supplies at a time—I already checked—so she won't have to worry about grabbing stuff every day. And I put some little plastic bags in there, too, so she can hide the used pull-ups before she throws them away in the morning."

He smiled. "Thanks for doing that."

"I just feel bad that she has so much to worry about, Mike."

"I do too, but I think you might be more worried than she is." He paused. "You might want to consider that, you know?"

"Yeah, maybe," I told him. But I wasn't sure I meant it.

‡ ‡

"So, what do you think you'll do all summer?" several friends asked me. "You're so lucky both kids are going away!"

"I'll probably sit next to the phone, in the fetal position, waiting for their camps to call and tell me to come pick up my kids."

"Seriously, Kate?" Michelle, my good friend and the therapist from my book club, responded. "Are you really that nervous about sending the kids to camp?"

"Yes. Sort of," I admitted. "Well, maybe. I don't know. I just want them both to love camp like I did."

"You can't really control whether they're gonna love it, Kate. You know that, right?"

"I know, but . . ."

"And you and Mike did the best jobs you could to find the right camps for both of your kids."

"I know."

"And now you just have to trust yourselves, your kids, and their camps that everything will be okay."

Easier said than done.

‡ ‡

I hardly slept the week before the kids left. Jacob's camp was scheduled to begin on a Saturday, and he'd leave by bus from the Upper East Side with about forty other New York City kids. Gabriella's camp started a day later, and in her case we'd drive her up, help her unpack, and then head home an hour or two later.

My heart raced during our drive across Central Park to Jacob's bus stop. The smile he'd woken up wearing that morning was now replaced with a furrowed brow. I wondered what my little Contemplator was thinking as we turned the corner to First Avenue and saw a mob of kids and parents congregating on the sidewalk.

As we got closer, it was easy to tell the pensive first-year campers from the chatting and laughing alums. It was also easy to tell that Jacob's discomfort level was rising.

"J-man, where are you going, buddy?" I asked as he walked away from the mob and turned down a side street.

"I don't want to go," he said.

"I bet you must be nervous, huh?"

"I don't want to go to camp." He started wiping his eyes. "What if no one talks to me?"

"Come here, buddy," I said, wrapping him in a bear hug. "I promise it's gonna be okay, Jacob. I promise. Plenty of kids will talk to you." We stood in silence for a few minutes, my arms still enveloping him. "Let's walk back to the bus, okay?"

"Okay, Mom," he said . . . and he looked up and flashed me a little half smile.

Twenty minutes later, Mike, Gabriella, and I waved as the bus pulled out and headed toward the George Washington Bridge.

One down, one to go, I thought.

‡ ‡

When we finally arrived at G's camp the next day and the counselors greeted us in the parking area to help us carry Gabriella's duffel bags to her bunk, it became abundantly clear that Gabriella had packed—or, more accurately, *I* had packed—more stuff than literally any other kid had brought to camp. No exaggeration. Our duffels dwarfed everyone else's. I blame the extra comforters. And sheets. And pull-ups. Not to mention the clear plastic crate I'd covered in duct tape to conceal the pull-ups. Truly, my kid could have been crowned "Most Overpacked Camper," with no second-place contender even coming close. I was glad, therefore, that we had arrived on the early side and could stake out some extra cubby space for her stuff.

"You okay, baby girl?" I asked her as we spread her comforter on the bottom bunk of one of the seven beds that lined her cabin.

"I'm fine, Mom," she said.

"Why don't we put up our pictures from home?" I suggested.

She looked around her area and frowned. "Where are we gonna put them?"

I looked around and realized there was not one shelf, cubby, or even hook anywhere near her bed. Apparently, each camper was allocated three small shelves in the back of the room and one drawer under their bed. (I found cobwebs in Gabriella's; I was immediately grateful I'd packed the wipes.)

"Not a problem," I told her. "We'll take the pictures out of the frames and tape them to your wall. Cool?"

"Cool."

Within thirty minutes, her area looked adorable—the emoji comforter, the "I Love Camp" rug/mat we'd put at the foot of her bed, and pictures of our family, her friends, and her and Gila taped to the wall.

While Gabriella and I unpacked and prepped her stuff, Mike stood outside with one of Gabriella's counselors. (We later learned that they identified as nonbinary; once again, we'd gotten incredibly lucky.) They went through the two pages of notes he'd typed and printed out listing Gabriella's medication schedule, "things to keep in mind," and all things pull-up related.

"So, did you make it through both pages?" I asked Mike and the counselor sarcastically when they rejoined us near Gabriella's bed.

The counselor laughed and nodded.

"We did indeed," Mike retorted. "Did you find space for everything in Gabriella's two ginormous duffel bags?"

"I did indeed," I told them. Though I left out the part where one of her counselors had helped me find some extra space in an adjoining bunk for the third comforter.

"Where's Gabriella?" I asked.

"No idea. Hmm . . ."

We checked the other beds, moved to the porch, and finally heard laughter coming from across the way. Gabriella had already found two of the girls she'd connected with back in New York and was playing a card game with them in the gazebo.

"Wow," I said, turning to Mike and then glancing back at our daughter.

Within another twenty minutes, Gabriella made it clear we were summarily dismissed. So, we did what any parents who'd spent only two nights alone together—and not consecutively—since we'd given birth would do: we hit the road and got the hell out of Dodge.

‡ ‡

On day four, we received letters from both kids. Jacob loved "his bunk and his counselors," and Gabriella was "having the best summer ever."

I exhaled. But just a little.

A brief email from Sari a couple days after that gave me another boost: "Gabriella is having tons of fun; she was a little homesick at first but has made lots of friends and is adjusting really well! Her counselors tell me she's a real chatterbox and keeps everyone smiling."

My insides started to relax; I declared the remaining weeks of July and August "The Summer of Kate and Mike." And it was. We rediscovered our city and our relationship—booked last-minute trips to Atlantic City, Upstate New York, and Washington, DC, and enjoyed every one.

I won't pretend things were perfect all summer, because they weren't. Not for the kids, and not for me and Mike. But I was okay with that—or at least learning to be.

By the sixth week, I couldn't wait for them to come home. I didn't stress about it, though; I didn't sit in the fetal position; and I didn't worry about making things "just right" for their return to our apartment. But I did look forward to having our family of four under the same roof again and going back to Myrtle Beach for the sixth consecutive summer—and the first with my son and daughter.

30: And They're Off!

"I wish I was back at camp!" That's what both kids told us repeatedly from just about the moment they got home until we left for Myrtle Beach. That gave us about a three-and-a-half-hour complaint reprieve, which Mike and I relished; as soon as we landed in South Carolina, however, their criticisms kicked in again, albeit in a slightly less aggressive fashion.

"It's a quality problem," Mike explained. "I'm so glad they both loved camp as much as they did!"

"I don't disagree," I said with a shrug.

And man, had they loved camp. Jacob was already counting down till the next summer, and Gabriella, who had originally objected to going for a full seven weeks, insisted that she needed to go for first and second session again next time.

I wasn't arguing. Not one bit. And I noticed the kids weren't arguing as much with each other either; perhaps absence does make the heart grow fonder, even with nine-year-old twins who historically haven't gotten along that well.

"Can we call George and Isabella now?" they both asked as soon as we made it to our condo.

"When are we going out for hibachi with them?" Gabriella asked.

"You know we *have* to go to hibachi again," Jacob said in his most convincing tone. "It's tradition, Mom and Dad. You know that."

"I do know that, Mr. Man. I do. And I'm sure we'll keep the tradition going strong this summer too."

"Okay," he said, nodding his little head. "Good."

‡ ‡

Jacob and Gabriella clicked extra well with George and Isabella this trip. As hard as it had been for Jacob to acknowledge that Gabriella was his sister, he seemed to have no problems thinking of George as one of the guys. And Gabriella and Isabella were two peas in a pod—they talked fashion, boys, jewelry, the whole stereotypically girlie gamut.

"You know, it's *almost* feeling like a vacation," I said to Mike one morning as we watched all the kids playing together on the beach. "I mean, don't get me wrong, it's still a 'trip,' but I could see how we might actually get a chance to relax at some point this week."

And then, as if on cue, we heard a loud, piercing, somewhat whiny "Jacob!" come from the water's edge and saw Jacob chasing after Gabriella with a pail full of water.

"Yeah, it's a trip all right," Mike said. And we both laughed.

‡ ‡

We arrived home on a Sunday evening, giving us three days to get the kids ready for school. Which seemed like a lot of time for some reason. I mean, sure, we had to do a couple loads of laundry, but beyond that, our normally packed calendar was uncharacteristically open.

What had changed? Was I not overscheduling us to keep myself distracted? Was my daughter no longer a project but simply a person?

A few days of playdates later and Jacob was headed back to school. Like the previous year, his school began a day earlier than Gabriella's. Unlike the previous year, I didn't send out a family update to the parents in his grade, nor did I lie awake worrying half the night before the big day. Also unlike the previous year, I woke up feeling rested and excited for his first day of school.

So, it seemed, did Jacob.

"Hey, Mommy and Daddy," he said, jumping into my and Mike's bed at about six fifteen that morning. "Are you getting ready to take me to school?"

"I was just about to jump in the shower, kiddo," I said, stifling a yawn. "Want pancakes for breakfast?"

"Okay," he said and then bounded into Gabriella's room, calling, "Gabriella, are you awake?"

"What a difference a year makes, huh?" I remarked to Mike as I headed to the shower.

"You're not kidding," he agreed.

‡ ‡

An hour and fifteen minutes later, Jacob, Mike, and I walked out of our building to go to school.

"Super J, can Dad grab a first-day picture of us?" I asked.

"Okay, but make it quick," Jacob replied. "I want to get to school early to see my friends."

Mike clicked away.

That year's "official" picture is still one of my favorites. My little man is rocking a beautiful bronze tan, newly coiffed haircut, his signature Yankees T-shirt, long baggy basketball shorts, and his new Steph Curry Under Armour backpack. I'm wearing one of my favorite Old Navy sundresses and sandals, and I'm clutching Jacob's shoulder with one hand and a cup of coffee with the other. What stands out most, though, is our smiles. I'm told we have similar smiles, but that's not what I'm referring to. Our smiles in the picture look genuine. We both seem relaxed. My son seems happy.

"First day of fourth grade for my not so little man! You got this, Super J."

That's the caption I put on Facebook as I posted the picture on our way to school. Mike and I walked Jacob to his class, introduced ourselves to his teachers, said hi to the other moms and dads, turned around, and headed home to Gabriella. No strained conversations. No stares—perceived or otherwise. Just your average, perfunctory first-day drop-off.

It felt amazing.

‡ ‡

The following day? I substituted Kid G for Kid J, swapped out my favorite Old Navy sundress with one from H&M, and grabbed a fresh coffee from the cart outside our building. The picture I asked Mike to take of me and G would also become one of my favorites.

"You sure you have your new shorts in your backpack, my love?" I asked Gabriella as we headed to school.

"I'm sure," she said, rolling her eyes.

She'd refused to wear the regulation-length cutoffs we'd made, opting instead for bright turquoise gym shorts that she slung low on her hips to make them look a little longer. (Mike and I insisted she bring her homemade cutoffs along in case her current shorts didn't pass the school's fingertip "dress code" test.) Mike held G's hand as we crossed Broadway, while I simultaneously walked and posted her annual first-day-of-school picture.

"And she's off!" my caption read. "First day of fourth grade for my beautiful daughter! Go get 'em, babe! #ProudMom."

A dear friend from college was the first to comment. I read her remark as we turned the final corner and approached Gabriella's no-longer-new school: "I especially love her T-shirt. So fitting. XO."

I glanced up, surprised I hadn't noticed her shirt before. It was the one her best friend Gila had given to her a few months earlier.

Plastered across the chest of the gray-and-white-speckled tie-dye was the phrase "Dreams do come true."

Yes, they do, I thought to myself as Mike and I kissed our daughter goodbye and watched as she smiled, waved, and walked into the building.

Notes

Chapter 3

1 Excerpts from "One of These Things (Is Not Like the Others)," by Joe Raposo & Bruce Hart, are reprinted with permission from The Joe Raposo Music Group.

2 Paul Raeburn, "Bullied Boy Allegedly Banned from Bringing 'My Little Pony' Backpack to School," TODAY, March 19, 2014, https://www.today.com/parents/bullied-boy-allegedly-banned-bringing-my-little-pony-backpack-school-2d79406114.

Chapter 4

1 From MY PRINCESS BOY by Cheryl Kilodavis. Text and illustrations copyright © 2009 by KD Talent LLC. Reprinted with the permission of Aladdin, an imprint of Simon & Schuster Children's Publishing Division. All rights reserved.

Chapter 7

1 Matt Donnelly, "Vanity Fair's Caitlyn Jenner Cover Scores Biggest Day in Site's History with Over 9 Million Unique Visitors," The Wrap, June 2, 2015, https://www.thewrap.com/vanity-fairs-caitlyn-jenner-cover-scores-sites-biggest-day-in-history-with-over-9-million-unique-visitors/.

2 Lena Dunham (@lenadunham), "I just want Caitlyn Jenner to

take me out and teach me how to drive a stick shift in heels," June 1, 2015, 10:43 a.m., https://twitter.com/lenadunham/status/605429578799153152.

3   https://www.mid-day.com/entertainment/hollywood-news/article/Barack-Obama--Hollywood-celebs-lend-support-to-Caitlyn-Jenner-16260164

4   Sara C. Nelson, "Caitlyn Jenner Mocked and Misgendered by Fox News Anchors Who Call Her Bruce," *Huffington Post*, June 2, 2015, https://www.huffingtonpost.co.uk/2015/06/02/caitlyn-jenner-mocked-misgendered-fox-news-anchors-bruce_n_7491452.html.

5   Emanuella Grinberg, "Why Caitlyn Jenner's Transgender Experience Is Far from the Norm," CNN Wires, June 3, 2015, https://fox2now.com/news/why-caitlyn-jenners-transgender-experience-is-far-from-the-norm/.

6   "Transgender Americans Experience Significant Economic, Health Challenges: Study," Vanderbilt University, April 13, 2020, https://news.vanderbilt.edu/2020/04/13/transgender-americans-experience-significant-economic-health-challenges-study/.

7   "New Study Reveals Shocking Rates of Attempted Suicide Among Trans Adolescents," Human Rights Campaign, September 12, 2018, https://www.hrc.org/news/new-study-reveals-shocking-rates-of-attempted-suicide-among-trans-adolescen.

Chapter 9

1   Nico Lang, "New Study: Rates of Anti-LGBTQ School Bullying at 'Unprecedented High,'" The Daily Beast, June 3, 2017, https://www.thedailybeast.com/new-study-rates-of-anti-lgbtq-school-bullying-at-unprecedented-high.

Chapter 11

1 Ryan Teague Beckwith, "Read Donald Trump's Speech on the Orlando Shooting," *TIME*, June 13, 2016, https://time.com/4367120/orlando-shooting-donald-trump-transcript/.

Chapter 12

1 "Trump's Timeline of Hate," Human Rights Campaign, https://www.hrc.org/resources/trumps-timeline-of-hate.

Chapter 13

1 "Interactive Map: Comprehensive Care Programs for Gender-Expansive Children and Adolescents," Human Rights Campaign, https://www.hrc.org/resources/interactive-map-clinical-care-programs-for-gender-nonconforming-childr.

Chapter 14

1 https://www.endocrine.org/news-and-advocacy/news-room/2020/transgender-teens-have-high-rates-of-depression-suicidal-thoughts

2 https://www.theguardian.com/society/2016/feb/26/crucial-study-transgender-children-mental-health-family-support

3 "Transgender Children & Youth: Understanding the Basics," Human Rights Campaign, https://www.hrc.org/resources/transgender-children-and-youth-understanding-the-basics.

Chapter 17

1 Albert E. Smith Jr., "On North Carolina's House Bill 2 (HB2): The Public Facilities Privacy and Security Act," National Institutes of Health, Office of Equity, Diversity, and Inclusion, April 18, 2016, https://www.edi.nih.gov/blog/news/north-carolinas-house-bill-2-hb2-public-facilities-privacy-and-security-act.

2 "Rep. Dan Bishop Rips Charlotte's 'Radical Transgender Proposal,'" *The Charlotte Observer*, January 20, 2016, https://www.wbtv.com/story/31007129/rep-dan-bishop-rips-charlottes-radical-transgender-proposal/.

3 "Rep. Dan Bishop Rips Charlotte's 'Radical Transgender Proposal.'"

4 https://www.newsobserver.com/article71238907.html

Chapter 20

1 Cole Park, "The Christian Right on the Gender Frontier: The Growing Anti-Trans Offensive," Political Research Associates, October 5, 2016, https://www.politicalresearch.org/2016/10/05/the-christian-right-on-the-gender-frontier-the-growing-anti-trans-offensive.

2 "Trump's Record of Action Against Transgender People," National Center for Transgender Equality, https://transequality.org/the-discrimination-administration.

Chapter 22

1 *Transgender and Gender Nonconforming Student Guidelines*, NYC Department of Education, March 1, 2017, https://static1.squarespace.com/static/5de2a8445511bf790e31e6e2/t/5df3a8e74c2e38505c089e1c/1576249575759/DOE-TransGNCGuidelinesMarch2017-1.pdf.

2 "New York City Issues New Guidelines to Protect Transgender Students," NYCLU, March 2, 2017, https://www.nyclu.org/en/press-releases/new-york-city-issues-new-guidelines-protect-transgender-students.

3 "LGBTQ Definitions," University of Colorado Boulder, Center for Inclusion and Social Change, https://www.colorado.edu/cisc/resources/trans-queer/lgbtq-definitions.

Chapter 23

1   Katie Rogers, "T.S.A. Defends Treatment of Transgender Air Traveler," *The New York Times*, September 22, 2015, https://www.nytimes.com/2015/09/23/us/shadi-petosky-tsa-transgender.html.

Chapter 24

1   Sarah McBride, "HRC & Trans People of Color Coalition Release Report on Violence Against the Transgender Community," Human Rights Campaign, November 17, 2017, https://www.hrc.org/news/hrc-trans-people-of-color-coalition-release-report-on-violence-against-the.

2   McBride, "HRC & Trans People of Color Coalition Release Report."

3   Madeline B. Deutsch, "Binding, Packing, and Tucking," UCSF Transgender Care, June 17, 2016, https://transcare.ucsf.edu/guidelines/binding-packing-and-tucking.

4   https://www.etsy.com/shop/LeoLines?utm_source=google&utm_medium=cpc&utm_campaign=Search_US_DSA_GGL_ENG_General-Nonbrand_Shop_Ext&utm_ag=UK-EN_DSA-Shop%252BPages&utm_custom1=_k_CjwKCAjw5dqgBhBNEiwA7PryaMX8azdEhgZgBJGdMLaiYYf-4OZUKHkz4NmihuIHt-eCdSE-VENPyRoCHKIQAvD_BwE_k_&utm_content=go_19243288493_143042704743_641284877485_aud-1184785539978:dsa-1640180280716_c_&utm_custom2=19243288493&gclid=CjwKCAjw5dqgBhBNEiwA7PryaMX8azdEhgZgBJGdMLaiYYf-4OZUKHkz4NmihuIHt-eCdSE-VENPyRoCHKIQAvD_BwE#reviews

Chapter 25

1   Jason J Westwater, Elizabeth Riley, and Gregory M. Peterson, "Using Circular Questions to Explore Individual Family Member Experiences of Youth Gender Dysphoria in Australia," *International Journal of Transgender Health* 21, no. 3 (June 12,

2020), https://www.tandfonline.com/doi/10.1080/26895269.2020
.1777616.

Chapter 26

1 Wikipedia, s.v. "LGBT Clergy in Judaism," last modified September 19, 2022, https://en.wikipedia.org/wiki/LGBT_clergy_in_Judaism.

2 "Resolution on the Rights of Transgender and Gender Nonconforming People," Union for Reform Judaism, 2015, https://urj.org/what-we-believe/resolutions/resolution-rights-transgender-and-gender-non-conforming-people.

3 "Orthodox Judaism and LGBTQ Issues," My Jewish Learning, https://www.myjewishlearning.com/article/orthodox-judaism-and-lgbtq-issues/.

4 "Stances of Faiths on LGBTQ Issues: Orthodox Judaism," Human Rights Campaign, https://www.hrc.org/resources/stances-of-faiths-on-lgbt-issues-orthodox-judaism.

5 Rahel Musleah, "Abby Stein Finds Her Voice," *Hadassah Magazine*, July 2020, https://www.hadassahmagazine.org/2020/07/08/abby-stein-finds-voice/.

Chapter 27

1 Sophie Tatum, "White House Announces Policy to Ban Most Transgender People from Serving in Military," CNN, March 24, 2018, https://www.cnn.com/2018/03/23/politics/transgender-white-house/index.html.

2 Sam Levin, "White House Announces Ban on Transgender People Serving in Military," *The Guardian*, March 24, 2018, https://www.theguardian.com/us-news/2018/mar/23/donald-trump-transgender-military-ban-white-house-memo.

3 "Name Changes and Forced Outing: A Small Victory," National Center for Transgender Equality, November 19, 2009,

https://transequality.org/blog/name-changes-and-forced-outing-a-small-victory.

4   "Name Changes and Forced Outing."

Chapter 28

1   "What Are Puberty Blockers?" Planned Parenthood, https://www.plannedparenthood.org/learn/teens/puberty/what-are-puberty-blockers.

2   "Precocious Puberty," Mayo Clinic, February 15, 2021, https://www.mayoclinic.org/diseases-conditions/precocious-puberty/symptoms-causes/syc-20351811.

3   Jack L Turban et al., "Pubertal Suppression for Transgender Youth and Risk of Suicidal Ideation," *Pediatrics* 145, no. 2 (February 2020), https://pediatrics.aappublications.org/content/145/2/e20191725.

Acknowledgments

As someone who craves instant gratification, writing this book was a lot like me trying to get pregnant- it didn't happen overnight, I needed to ask for help, and the process was significantly more challenging than I expected.

"What do you mean, it's not done yet?"

"Really...dig deeper? I thought I already did that!"

"I can't just quote the song and credit the writer? I need to submit a 'permission request' and wait for a response?"

Yup, this whole "book thing" was both a journey and a learning experience. And just like becoming a parent, I'm incredibly grateful I took the leap and incredibly thankful for my posse, who ultimately helped me birth this baby.

Thank you to my husband for your love and unwavering support, for helping to create our perfectly imperfect family, for putting down your spreadsheets long enough to hear me read (and re-read) sentences, paragraphs, and chapters to you over and over...and over again. I love you! Today. Tomorrow. Always.

To my rock star kids, for making me a mom, for making me the *proudest* mom, for being brave, and most of all, for being you. I love you more than I ever thought I could love. Now, please, can I just take a nap?

To my bro (a.k.a. King Slickness), for teaching me how to throw a spiral, for not killing me during my "mean years", for finally understanding that I have no desire to try P90X ("Which way to the beach?"), and for being the best big brother, supporter, and friend to your "ninth court master slickness in training." I love you!

To my dad and stepmom for dealing with my (previous) bad hair days, bad mood days, and bad taste days (bad taste in clothes, jobs, boys, and just about everything else). But most of all, thank you for loving me, for ALWAYS being there for me and my family, and for being the best nana and papa ever…period.

To my mom, with whom I had an incredibly complicated relationship and who I loved… and still love, wholeheartedly. You never got the chance to meet your youngest granddaughter, but somehow, I think "you knew." (P.S. God, you would be so proud of these kids!)

To NK/NW, for believing in me and this book even when it was "Swiss cheese," for editing and re-editing my copy, for holding my hand during the "find an agent, sign with an agent, drop an agent" process, for helping me navigate the wonky world that is publishing, and for becoming a cherished friend.

To HB, AB, JB, and GB, our favorite family in Myrtle Beach and beyond! What are the chances? No, really, what are the actual chances of us finding one another at some random resort in one of the reddest states? I would say we should all go out and play the lottery but having friends like you—with whom we can laugh, cry, swim, sun, sip, and share, we've already won. Corny? Yes. Accurate? 100%. We are incredibly grateful to be on this journey together.

To my besties, THANK YOU for your love, support, guidance, laughter, and happy hours over the years, especially the last few. KO, VS, JK, SL, MC, SS, LS, AH, TS, ELP, KD, AS, JW, AP, SH, MM, BG, and so many others. I love you. I appreciate you. I'm grateful to you. And…I hope you can convince people to buy this book!

Thank you to SL, LK, and the entire CRS clergy, who are my rabbis, cantors, community, and friends. For welcoming, embracing, and supporting our family at every turn; for (SL) suggesting the perfect title for this book and meeting with me straight from your Soul Cycle workout; for (BS) offering the best hugs (how did you ever survive covid?); for (SDL) holding my daughter's hand during her first Aliyah; and to all of you, for holding our family whenever we needed holding.

To JM, BD, and all my peeps at GFP for reminding me that my family and I are not alone, for teaching me how to advocate for my daughter, and for providing a safe haven for so many kids and caregivers. "I think I'll take 'life-raft' for a million dollars, Alex."

Thank you to my daughter's incredible gender therapist, whom I'd love to mention by name, but will refrain from doing so to protect her and her awesome program from the haters. Wow, our kiddo is so lucky to have you in her corner, but then again, so is our whole family.

To ZC for being the best (and most beautiful) role model and friend to me and my daughter and for making sure our hair looks fabulous! I'm so glad I randomly walked into your salon that day, and I'm supremely grateful you didn't wake up in Spain missing a kidney.

To BW, LW, KL, BB, KA, and the rest of the team at She Writes Press (my fellow writers included), thank you for your support, your sisterhood, your belief in me and my project, and for not killing me during the cover design process. (Umm, would you like me to share more font suggestions?)

And finally, and most importantly, to every transgender, gender non-conforming and/or gender questioning person out there... please know you are loved, you *have* value and *are* valued, and you deserve to live a happy, healthy, authentic, and SAFE life. And my posse and me?? We'll always have your backs.

About the Author

photo credit: Sarah Merians

Kate Brookes is an award-winning TV reporter/anchor-turned-producer/filmmaker who has interviewed everyone from Beyonce to Barbara Walters, field produced for The Discovery Channel, written for Today.com, and emceed galas, live events, and webcasts for nonprofits and Fortune 500 companies. An activist since her teenage years, Kate has devoted countless hours to the causes she supports, including mental health, housing justice, and anti-gun legislation. But it wasn't until realizing she'd completely botched the birth announcement for her twins that she became active in LGBTQ causes. Kate lives with her husband and rock star children in New York City.

SELECTED TITLES FROM SHE WRITES PRESS

She Writes Press is an independent publishing company founded to serve women writers everywhere. Visit us at www.shewritespress.com.

Once a Girl, Always a Boy: A Family Memoir of a Transgender Journey by Jo Ivester. $16.95, 978-1-63152-886-6

Thirty years ago, Jeremy Ivester's parents welcomed him into the world as what they thought was their daughter. Here, his mother—with Jeremy's help—chronicles his journey from childhood through coming out as transgender and eventually emerging as an advocate for the transgender community.

Handsome: Stories of an Awkward ~~Girl Boy~~ Human by Holly Lorka $16.95, 978-1-63152-783-8

As a horny little kid, Holly Lorka had no idea why God had put her in the wrong body and made her want to kiss girls. She had questions: Was she a monster? Would she ever be able to grow sideburns? And most importantly, where was her penis? Here, she tells the story of her romp through the first fifty years of her life searching for sex, love, acceptance, and answers to her questions.

You Can't Buy Love Like That: Growing Up Gay in the Sixties by Carol E. Anderson. $16.95, 978-1631523144

A young lesbian girl grows beyond fear to fearlessness as she comes of age in the '60s amid religious, social, and legal barriers.

The Doctor and The Stork: A Memoir of Modern Medical Babymaking by K.K. Goldberg. $16.95, 978-1-63152-830-9

A mother's compelling story of her post-IVF, high-risk pregnancy with twins—the very definition of a modern medical babymaking experience.

Parent Deleted: A Mother's Fight for Her Right to Parent by Michelle Darné. $16.95, 978-1-63152-282-6

A gripping tale of one non-biological, lesbian mother's fight for shared custody of her children—an intimate, infuriating, and infectious story of perseverance, sacrifice, and hope in the face of debilitating adversity.